MW00939838

Acknowledgments

I would like to thank everyone who has assisted me with this book. I'm thankful for my beautiful wife, Nikki, who has always encouraged me with my book projects. Thank you, Warren and Paula Berkley, for all the time you have put in and being a sounding board for me. A special thanks to all the preachers who answered so many questions. I'm thankful you all have dedicated your lives preaching the gospel of Jesus Christ. May God bless you in all you do. Most importantly, I'm thankful to God and His Son Jesus Christ. It's not about us. It's all about them. To God be the glory. God is good not just some of the time, but all the time God is good.

Cover design by Left Align Creative
Kindle formatting by Paula Berkley

Table of Contents

Page

Introduction

One of the best decisions I've made in my life was to be a part of the Dowlen Road church of Christ preacher-training program. It was 2008 when I first heard about the two-year program. At that time, I was working with Pfizer Pharmaceuticals as a sales representative. I was ready for a change. My wife and I had moved to Columbia, MO. I had preached occasionally while we were living in Rockford, IL. I had thought about preaching full time for a long time. While I had thought about it, I knew that I wasn't ready.

During our second year in Columbia, MO, an opportunity opened. The preacher at our congregation left. The church was looking for someone to fill in and preach until they found a full-time worker. Another brother and I were asked if we would preach. I was really excited about this opportunity. Full discloser: I had no idea what I was doing. It's hard for me to even listen to the sermons that I presented there. But I was up for the challenge. The brethren were patient with me. I'm thankful they were. I was still working full time with Pfizer and preaching 2–3 times per month.

By 2008, I knew a couple of things. First, I knew I wanted to get into preaching full time. Second, I was probably going to lose my job with Pfizer. I began to think about my exit strategy. I knew I wanted to preach, but I didn't know what direction to go. I needed some guidance. I prayed. My wife and I talked about where we could potentially go. I was thinking about going back to college to get a degree in Biblical studies. But then something happened. I reached out to the elders at our congregation. I'm so glad that I did. They were the ones who recommended I reach out to the brethren in Beaumont, TX. I had never heard of Beaumont, TX, until 2008. Could anything good come out of Beaumont, TX? Yes!

I spoke with Max Dawson and David Banning about the preacher-training program there. It just so happened they were looking for a young man for the program. I was a little older than previous trainees. But they wanted us to come and visit. The weekend went great. We spoke with the elders and other brethren. Eventually, they asked if we wanted to be a part of the program. We said yes. But there was something else to figure out. I was still employed with Pfizer. It just so happened that there was going to be a big cut of employees beginning in January 2009. Everyone was nervous about keeping their job, except for me. I prayed I would get severed. I would get a nice severance package, which would help us since there would be a steep pay cut going into the training program. I asked the brethren in Missouri to pray I would get let go. I got a lot of stares from them about this request. But our prayers would be answered. I was let go by the company. We left Columbia, MO, and began the training program on July 2, 2009. That was one of the best decisions of our lives. I believe God was at work.

Speaking to the elders played a big role getting us to Beaumont, TX. There was someone else who also played a big role. It was one of my doctors. He gave me a book called *Rich Dad, Poor Dad*. In the book, the author talked a lot about how his Rich Dad surrounded himself with people smarter than him. That stuck with me as I thought about the training program in Beaumont. Max Dawson and David Banning had decades of preaching experience. I didn't. I knew I could learn from them. So, I decided I wanted to learn from them. I didn't want to be 40 and regret not at least giving preaching a chance. I would have rather failed than not tried. During those two years at Dowlen Road, I learned how to do the work of a preacher well. I'm thankful I was able to spend almost nine years at Dowlen Road (two as a trainee and six and a half as a full-time worker). But I didn't merely learn from Max and David. I learned from the shepherds at the congregation about what leadership looks like. I learned from other preachers like Don Swanson. Don invited me to work with him three days a week in Liberty, TX, while I was in the training program. That was a great experience as I learned a great deal about personal work. I learned from men like Mark Roberts and Warren Berkley when I attended their Young Preachers Workshops.

So, where I am going with all of this? I've been blessed to have mentors like Max and David and many others for the past decade. There's great benefit being able to learn from others.

It's better to LEARN and LIVE instead of LIVE and LEARN. When we open up our Bibles we see:

- The apostles learned from Jesus. They needed His guidance.
- Timothy and Titus were able to learn from the apostle Paul, 1 Timothy 1:1-2.
- Joshua was able to learn from Moses. In Exodus 17:14, it says, "Then the LORD said to Moses, 'Write this as a memorial in a book and recite it in the ears of Joshua, that I will utterly blot out the memory of Amalek from under heaven." Moses was a mentor to Joshua. In Exodus 24:13, it says, "So Moses rose with his assistant Joshua, and Moses went up into the mountains of God." Joshua was able to learn a great deal from Moses by being his assistant.

The list could go on and on. There's great benefit learning from others.

Now I want to be clear about something. The one that we need to listen to the most is God and His Son Jesus Christ. They have all authority, not men, Matthew 28:19-20. We need to listen to the words of the Holy Spirit, 2 Timothy 3:16. Paul said, "All Scripture is breathed out by God and profitable for teaching, for reproof, for correction, and for training in righteousness, that the man of God may be complete, equipped for every good work." A man who desires to be a preacher needs to turn first and foremost to the Holy Scriptures. Men can be wrong. God is never wrong.

At the same time, there is benefit of learning from others. There's benefit of having a mentor, working next to someone, learning how to do things well, so that God can be glorified. As Christians and as preachers we want to strive for excellence in all we do. WHY? So people will know the true and living God.

One morning I had an idea. I was reading a book where the author reached out to people he respected seeking answers to questions about life. As I was reading, I was fascinated with the information he was able to collect just by asking people questions. A few weeks earlier I had the opportunity to meet a preacher named Ken Weliever. When I walked into his office I saw something on his wall. He had photos of men who had played a big role to him as a preacher. He described them as his cloud of witnesses. Seeing that wall and hearing those words combined with the book I was reading got me thinking of something.

What if there was a way for me to create a book where I could reach out to a number of preachers around the country where I could learn from them? What if young men who are not able to go into a preacher training program, like I did, had a resource where they could learn from other preachers with more experience? I was really excited about the idea. I reached out to Warren Berkley and ran the idea past him. He liked the idea. That conversation has led to this book.

This book is designed for you to learn from other preachers. Again, it's not to replace God's word. God's word is always our authority. But it is designed to demonstrate good habits from other preachers. It's designed to give you ideas or suggestions that could help you to become even more productive in God's kingdom.

Warren and I reached out to a number of preachers across the country. We gave them a list of 16 questions to reply. We then put those questions and answers in this book for you to have as a resource. The answers from the preachers have been organized by alphabetical according to last names:

1. Matt Bassford
2. Jarod Bollman
3. Warren Berkley
4. Jeff Carr
5. Caleb Churchill
6. Brady Cook
7. Chris Eppler
8. Ryan Goodwin
9. Robert Harkrider
10. Shawn Jeffries
11. Benjamin Lee
12. Justin McCorkle
13. Shane Millard
14. Brent Moody
15. David Osteen
16. Gabriel Puente
17. Bruce Reeves
18. Warren Scholtz
19. Don Swanson
20. Ken Weliever

Matt Bassford

1. *How and when did you decide to get into preaching full time? What was your motivation or your WHY?*

   I decided to try my hand at preaching in May 2004. At that point, I had been trying and failing to find work as a lawyer for about a year; and after a conversation with my brother, I realized that my forthright discussion of my faith in job interviews was the reason why. I decided that if talking about my convictions would be a problem as a lawyer, I ought to try work in which talking about my convictions was beneficial.

2. *As a preacher, have you always worked in a full-time setting capacity or have you been like Paul building tents from time to time?*

   Always full time.

3. *What one piece of advice would you give a young man who has begun to preach?*

   Work hard. It's easy for a preacher to slack off and be a mediocre servant, but God deserves excellence. There are men who have the ability to preach a great sermon off the cuff, but generally, they can't reach those heights consistently. Practice and preparation make a preacher consistently useful in the pulpit.

4. *What wisdom would you give a young man who was thinking about getting into preaching? How can one know when to pull the plug with their decision?*

   Be honest with yourself. If there is something you love more than proclaiming the gospel, do that instead.

5. *How do you start your mornings to maximize your day?*

   I get up at 6:30, exercise, get ready for the day, and then meet with my co-worker at about 8:45 for an hour and a half of Bible study and discussion of our work.

6. *How do you start your week to maximize your time?*

I work Mondays, coming in to the office at the same time. It can be hard, especially if the day before was a demanding Sunday, but I like being done with my work by Saturday so I can spend the day with my family.

7. *What's the biggest challenge you've faced as a preacher? How did you handle it?*

The biggest challenge I've faced as a preacher were some difficult relationships with other Christians in my previous work. I handled the situation by 1) concluding that it was time to move on, 2) doing my best to keep a lid on the problems so as not to disrupt the unity of the congregation, and 3) resolving the personal problems before I left.

8. *How does your wife help you in your ministry?*

Immensely. She's an extrovert's extrovert, a real people person. She's very outgoing and friendly with members and visitors alike, she loves to entertain, and she's a strong Bible student who contributes usefully in classes and kitchen-table studies. I also turn to her for advice more than I turn to anybody else. She truly is a Priscilla to my Aquila!

9. *How do you go about writing a sermon? Topic? Length?*

These days, many of my sermon topics come from discussions with my co-worker. We try to use our preaching to meet the spiritual needs we see in the congregation. I try to make sure that I spell out the applications of the principles I preach. Length-wise, I aim for 25–30 minutes.

In terms of process, I scratch out an outline, then write a full-sentence manuscript that I use in preparation (though I don't actually have it with me in the pulpit).

10. *What book have you gifted the most to people?*

The Bible! For a while, I kept a stack of Bibles with the same page numbering as mine to distribute to outsiders I was studying with who didn't know Genesis from Revelation. I don't do this as much these days because most people will pull the Bible up on a smartphone app, for which no previous knowledge is required.

11. *What are some of your favorite books to read?*

Again, the Bible! Seriously, I'm a big believer in daily Bible reading and have been reading through the Bible yearly for several years now. Other than that, I will read the occasional religiously oriented book, but most of my reading is for pleasure. Science fiction, fantasy, historical novels, histories, and biographies make up the bulk of it. I think reading history and biographies is particularly useful because of the insight it can give me into human nature.

12. *When do you know when it's time to move to another work?*

When I feel like I've lost effectiveness. In real life, every church has a ceiling, a point beyond which you cannot take them. When you reach that point, it's probably better to yield your place to another worker with a different approach. He may be able to accomplish things you couldn't.

13. *What advice would you give to other preachers when it comes to work/family balance?*

Just because preaching is a good work doesn't mean that it is the only good work. Loving my wife as Christ loved the church is a good work too. So is bringing up my children in the discipline and instruction of the Lord. If my work as a preacher is hindering my ability to fulfill God's expectations in those other areas, something has to change. That might mean saying no to some opportunity, but I don't want to be the preacher who wins the world and loses his family.

14. *Timothy had Paul as a mentor. Who was or is your Paul in the faith? In what ways were they able to help you?*

I had two mentors in the preacher-training program at the Dowlen Road church in Beaumont, TX: Max Dawson and David Banning. I was in the program for 18 months, and during that time, they equipped me with everything they thought I needed to succeed as a preacher. Once I got out on my own, I learned the value of everything they had taught me. To this day, whenever I need help or advice in some aspect of my work, I will turn to them.

15. *What piece of advice would you give when it comes to evangelism?*

The key to evangelism is loving people, caring about souls, and getting involved in the lives of others. Through the years, Lauren and I have found that it helps a great deal when we make a point of eating with outsiders before we study with them. When we extend hospitality to others, it shows them that we care about them and gives them the opportunity to get to know us and develop a relationship with us. It's a whole lot easier to study the Bible with someone who knows and trusts you than with somebody who doesn't.

16. *How do you decide how many meetings to hold? When should you decline invitations? How do you go about declining invitations?*

I don't get a whole lot of meeting invitations (1–2 a year), so this doesn't really come up a whole lot. I pretty much accept all the invitations that I get.

Currently, Matt Bassford works with the Jackson Heights church in Columbia, TN, where he has been for a whopping 10 months!

Jared Bollman

1. *How and when did you decide to get into preaching full time? What was your motivation or your WHY?*

The why is easy. I was surrounded by great influences. I grew up with parents who had a passion for the Bible. It was part of our life. I grew up hearing Dee Bowman preach every Sunday. He lit a fire. I grew up with great Bible class teachers. People like Bruce Turner, Philip and Karen Stover, Victor Estes, and so many others who had a passion for inspiring the young. Preaching felt like breathing. It was just what needed to be. *How* was a bit of a winding road. At first, I worked with smaller congregations. For 15 years, I tried to keep up a nearly impossible schedule of working full time at preaching and maintaining a professional secular career as well. You learn after a time that it's impossible to devote yourself entirely to two things. I applaud anyone who is willing to give of themselves in this way. May the Lord bless them all, but for me, I could never devote myself as fully to it as I needed to. So, I stepped away from preaching for a time. I threw myself into teaching Bible classes, writing articles, and filling in for Tony Mauck. When another opportunity came, I said goodbye to my 20-year career and moved to Centerville.

2. *As a preacher, have you always worked in a full-time setting capacity or have you been like Paul building tents from time to time?*

I've been a full-time tent maker, and it's not easy. If I could offer one piece of advice here, it would be this: Don't let the career that allows you to preach become the crutch that keeps you from doing more of the work. God bless every tent maker out there. They deserve our thanks. But don't be afraid to launch out. If you are making tents today, I salute you for it. Don't lose the fire.

3. *What one piece of advice would you give a young man who has begun to preach?*

I'm so glad you asked. It's not about who you like or who doesn't like you (they'll be plenty of both), you love them all the same. It isn't about what you want to preach. If your sermons fit the needs of the people, you'll be loved by some, hated by others, praised, and castigated. That's good. It means they found the mark. Every sermon needs a reason to exist beyond a passing selfish interest. If you don't have a purpose for preaching it, they'll wonder why they are hearing it.

4. *What wisdom would you give a young man who was thinking about getting into preaching? How can one know when to pull the plug with their decision?*

   Don't do it...until you know why. Don't kick tires; people love the preacher. Don't betray that trust by seeing if you like it. Preaching needs to be a passion, not a vague hobby. **Make sure your why is powerful.** People are fragile. Don't break their hearts.

5. *How do you start your mornings to maximize your day?*

   Sermon prep is the thing we all want to get to, but I never start my mornings that way; most of my sermon prep is done in the evening after my son is in bed. My mind is sharper then. Before I do anything, I try to take a few minutes and figure out what is today going to be about. You won't get much out of a day if you're reacting to everything. Next comes reading, articles commentaries, the scripture, anything to get the mind working and digesting information. After that, I spend a lot of time saying no until I find something that needs a yes. People always know how to spend your time better than you do; don't let them.

6. *How do you start your week to maximize your time?*

   I listen to Ben Lee, and then I wish I was more like him. I don't keep a rigid weekly structure. I wish I did, but I don't. You have to decide what kind of preacher you're going to be. I write all my class material that takes a lot of time. I host a class in my house every Thursday that also takes time. Time is the one thing you can't buy more of. You have to choose how you will invest yours. Prioritize, and make sure you are living up to your obligations, and if you find yourself not meeting goals or deadline, figure out where you're losing time. Be honest, are you taking on too much, spending too much time checking Facebook, are you allowing too many interruptions?

7. *What's the biggest challenge you've faced as a preacher? How did you handle it?*

Wow, talk about an open field. Not to sound cliché, but the biggest challenge is always the one you don't know exists yet. Whether it's the long hard look in the mirror and realizing I needed to change, the congregation that's just barely holding on after a division, or launching out and working for the first time without a career as a safety net; life is 10 percent what happens to you and 90 percent what you are willing to do about it. From attitude to application, approach everything with prayer and with a desire to please God. When the challenge comes from other people, don't forget you love them. Even if they don't love you, remember it's not about you.

8. *How does your wife help you in your ministry?*

In every way imaginable, but mostly because she makes me see the world as an extrovert and reminds me what people need from me.

9. *How do you go about writing a sermon? Topic? Length?*

Several years ago, I started preaching on yearly themes. It builds a lot of your material for you, and the people know what to expect. I do a lot of series work because people need repetition. As for topics, I try to stay away from what everyone is talking about unless I have a reason to be talking about it. Everyone knows abortion is bad, homosexuality is a sin, and adultery shouldn't happen. I am not going to give a sermon on those things if they aren't the needs of the people. However, I will preach on grace 12 times in a year because many people don't have a clue how it applies to them.

How I write a sermon is pretty basic. I start with a passage or a topic I read. For a topical sermon, I always start with an anchor passage that addresses the topic and then build the sermon following the structure of the passage. Even my topical sermons go through an expository evolution. Length is a whole other story. You have to figure out what works. People are too caught up in sermon length. I've preached sermons that lasted just over 19 minutes and others that have gone over an hour; both were well received. If you have a track record of being succinct, engaging, and straightforward, people will give you a lot of grace when you need more time. Don't waste their time.

10. *What book have you gifted the most to people?*

The Bible; *Understanding Apocalyptic Literature: a Guide to the Book of Revelation* by Mark Roberts.

11. *What are some of your favorite books to read?*

I read everything and anything. It's one of the reasons I keep Kris Emerson on speed dial. He's always reading something great. I love a good commentary especially when it challenges me to think differently about a passage; something motivational, but don't forget to read the Bible, not just for prep and study—make it a passion.

12. *When do you know when it's time to move to another work?*

I'll let you know. I worry about being effective. I don't want to waste people's time. Preaching is not about personality but growth. If the people aren't growing, then it's time to change tactics. If they still aren't growing, then maybe it's time to change preachers. When conflicts arise, try to work through them with humility. Pride is the undoing of so many men today; don't become one of them. When a situation becomes unworkable, don't allow it to envelop and divide others. Be open with your elders about what's going on.

13. *What advice would you give to other preachers when it comes to work/family balance?*

You are uniquely blessed, don't cheat the brethren. Give them what they need from their preacher. (This comes from Mark Roberts, so it's probably the smartest thing I've said.)

14. *Timothy had Paul as a mentor. Who was or is your Paul in the faith? In what ways were they able to help you?*

The traditional mentoring relationship wasn't in the cards for me, but there are men from whom I have learned much. Dee Bowman, whether he knew it or not was like a north star for me. My dad, he made tents for a lot of years. Most of the encouragement I got in the early years was from him. In recent years, I've gained a lot from Warren Berkley. He and Mark Roberts do a lot for guys that are trying to hone their craft. Everyone needs a Warren to give them the unvarnished truth.

Tony Mauck is the guy though. Tony is my one-on-one guy. He's the one who I can pick up the phone and talk things through. He's the one who looked at me after worshipping together for almost three years and asked, "What are you still doing here?"

On this note, find your Proverbs 27:17 guys. These are not mentors, but friends who keep you sharp. Kris Emerson and Ben Lee are my go-to here. We are nothing alike, and that's why I need them. They challenge me in the areas where I'm not sharp. I see what they do, and I want to do better. I hope they get the same from me. Find your irons, find a lot of them, and use them. Find a David Osteen, or a Jeremy Hodges, someone who isn't like you and opens your eyes, but through all of it, remember that the goal is not imitation but encouragement.

15. *What piece of advice would you give when it comes to evangelism?*

Learn the difference between evangelism and arguing. Practice the one and stop doing the other. Be personable. No one cares what you know about the Bible until they know that you care.

16. *How do you decide how many meetings to hold? When should you decline invitations? How do you go about declining invitations?*

Meetings are the icing on the cake. They taste great but too many, and it all goes to the waistline (literally). Listen to your elders on how many. The congregation is your priority. Don't lose sight of the people at home. I haven't declined any meetings other than for scheduling. When declining, I always start with the words I'm sorry and thank you.

Preaching for nearly 20 years, Jared has worked with congregations in Mexico, Houston, and Centerville, TX. In 2014, he left his secular work and began laboring full-time with the church in Centerville, where he serves as the local evangelist. Aside from pulpit work, Jared teaches a weekly Bible class in the family's home entitled Fundamentals of Faith. Currently, he is developing detailed class material for each book of the Bible with the aim of producing a set of simple approachable commentaries for people who wish to better understand God's word, and has begun working on a set of novels meant to be shared between fathers and sons that teach biblical principles in narrative form. Jared and Lauren married in 2003, and in 2014, they welcomed their newborn son William into their home, finalizing the adoption later that year.

Warren Berkley

1. *How and when did you decide to get into preaching full time? What was your motivation or your WHY?*

   I was raised in a home with an emphasis on the Lord and His work, so I always thought about preaching but didn't consider myself sufficient for the task. I was pushed by my wife's uncle (Lewis Willis, a gospel preacher) and gradually figured out, indeed I am not sufficient for the task but He is (2 Corinthians 3:5). I did part-time preaching while in college, then made the choice to go full-time after college. Motivation? I believed I could and should.

2. *As a preacher, have you always worked in a full-time setting capacity or have you been like Paul building tents from time to time?*

   I honor tent-makers and consider them an important part of Kingdom work. I, however, have been engaged full-time for the majority of my preaching life.

3. *What one piece of advice would you give a young man who has begun to preach?*

   Immerse yourself in the Word. I have often said to young men, there are four things you have to know to be a faithful preacher: (1) The Lord, (2) His Word, (3) Yourself, and (4) The people.

4. *What wisdom would you give a young man who was thinking about getting into preaching? How can one know when to pull the plug with their decision?*

   Resist typical ambitions to make a name for yourself. Read and study your Bible with such reverence and intent, the Word first becomes a part of you, then you share it as effectively as you are able.

5. *How do you start your mornings to maximize your day?*

   Awake at 6; pray while still in bed before turning anything on. Breakfast with wife, at my desk before 8.

6. *How do you start your week to maximize your time?*

   Monday mornings, I spend up to 20 minutes or so just mapping out the week, looking at the calendar, checking the memo list of things left undone, and considering calls and appointments.

7. *What's the biggest challenge you've faced as a preacher? How did you handle it?*

   The biggest and most recent challenge—making the transition to elder, while still being the local preacher. I faced it with good support from my wife, consulting my advisors/friends, encouragement from the other elder here, and prayer. I'll be working on wearing both these hats as long as I serve in both capacities.

8. *How does your wife help you in your ministry?*

   There isn't anyone on earth I depend on more than my wife, for encouragement, advise, listening, and helping me arrange my schedule. She wants me to do this and never complains.

9. *How do you go about writing a sermon? Topic? Length?*

   Once I have a passage/topic, I write down first thoughts then let that marinate a few days. Go back and revisit, adding additional thoughts; then do reading and research, which always results in further revisions, sometimes a complete change in direction. Then outline and write the first draft adding flesh (details) to the outline, illustrations, quotations, etc. I like to have a day or two before final draft to think, pray, revise. My outlines are virtual manuscripts. Sermons are generally 25–30 minutes.

10. *What book have you gifted the most to people?*

    Letters to Young Preachers.

11. *What are some of your favorite books to read?*

    Any books written by Gary Henry, Paul Earnhart, or Dee Bowman.

12. *When do you know when it's time to move to another work?*

Since I've been in McAllen for 29 years, I've forgotten any little wisdom I ever had about when to move!

13. *What advice would you give to other preachers when it comes to work/family balance?*

Family first!

14. *Timothy had Paul as a mentor. Who was or is your Paul in the faith? In what ways were they able to help you?*

My father died when I was 13, but his example has been before me every day. Lewis Willis really helped me get started simply with encouragement and necessary correction. Dee Bowman and Mark Roberts are powerful influences.

15. *What piece of advice would you give when it comes to evangelism?*

Make an effort to get out of your office regularly and widen your circle of friends. Don't let anyone tell you this is just your job; every Christian should be talking to others about the Lord.

16. *How do you decide how many meetings to hold? When should you decline invitations? How do you go about declining invitations?*

I've never really had a fixed plan about meetings. I thought they were "to be desired to make one wise" or something early in my preaching. I hold an average of four a year, and when I'm asked beyond what I'm booked already, I just say "sorry, you'll have to push me later in your planning." A few times I've told brethren, "I am just not the man you need for what you have planned."

Warren Berkley has been preaching for nearly 50 years. He graduated from the University of Arkansas Fort Smith. His family of three children and eight grandchildren have supported him through many local church works: Etna, AR; Waldron, AR; Mulvane, KS; Highlands, TX; and McAllen, TX.

Warren was the front page editor of *Preceptor* for 10 years, author of several *Quest for Truth* tracts, associate editor of *Pressing On* magazine, co-editor of *Expository Files*, and general editor and associate editor of several books. For 12 years, he has worked with Mark Roberts in the Young Preachers Workshop in Irving, TX.

Jeff Carr

1. *How and when did you decide to get into preaching full time? What was your motivation or your WHY?*

I did not grow up in a Christian home. While working on a degree in history with intentions of teaching at the high school or college level, I felt that I had tried just everything in life and was unsatisfied. Plus, I realized I had sinned and nothing remedied that. At the age of 23, I decided to search for something non-denominational and found a local church of Christ in the yellow pages. I walked in off the street into the Folsom church of Christ (Folsom, CA) and never turned back. Within three months, I became a Christian at the age of 23. I soon began teaching and preaching. Why I preach? It was either preach the gospel or teach history, which parallel each other. I do NOT want anyone to miss out on what I missed out on for so much of my life. I see the benefits of God's grace and forgiveness, and how the Bible can make sense in a chaotic world.

2. *As a preacher, have you always worked in a full-time setting capacity or have you been like Paul building tents from time to time?*

I was fortunate enough (blessed) to find a wonderful preacher-training program at the Country Club Rd. church of Christ (Tucson, AZ) and I was their fourth person they put through their formal training program under the preacher Hugh DeLong. That was a valuable asset to me. I stayed there 1.5 years. Bro. DeLong still serves as a mentor to me in many ways over the last 20 years. I hope to pay it forward by one day running my own preacher training program. Since I left Tucson, I have been a full-time preacher ever since. I have taken up small jobs here and there but the focus is the gospel. I have been fortunate (blessed) to be fully supported in doing this.

3. *What one piece of advice would you give a young man who has begun to preach?*

I would offer the same advice to any young person that was the same advice given to me. One, don't be afraid to wear out the seat of your pants doing some studying! Two, be yourself. Put the Word of God in your heart and let that speak for itself. Don't let your personality or bad motives get in the way of His inspired Word (1 Corinthians 2:1). Listen to those who criticize and allow that to keep you humble (2 Corinthians 12:7, James 1:2f). Make sure you find a good friend, or two (or more) that you can lean on as an ombudsman. You should always have the goal of improvement-improvement in Bible knowledge, in sermon preparation, in public speaking (join a local Toastmasters club for example), etc. Make sure you find a good friend who can give you the straight truth on how you are doing without being overly critical of you. We all need an ombudsman in our lives!

4. *What wisdom would you give a young man who was thinking about getting into preaching? How can one know when to pull the plug with their decision?*

Make sure you are following 1 Thessalonians 5:17.

One should NOT get into full-time preaching simply because there is nothing else to do. Make sure you check your motives to make sure they are pure and right. Do you have a desire to save souls? Do you have a desire to preserve souls that are already saved? Are you disciplined enough to have a flexible schedule? Are you able to juggle multiple tasks and still get things done and meet deadlines? Are you ready to expect the unexpected? For example, you can set out your whole week for study and classes and you never know when a person might walk into your office and want to talk for a few hours. Are you ready to live in a fishbowl and is your family ready for that? Do you have thick skin because sometimes the criticism will be unfair? Do you have humility because sometimes the compliments will be over the top?

5. *How do you start your mornings to maximize your day?*

I try to go to bed early so I can arise early each morning. The first thing I like to do when I wake up is pray and study. I find that my mind is fresh and clear early in the morning and is not drowned out by the effluvia of noise that can occupy our day. I can be very productive before the world wakes up and starts crowding me out on my phone, on social media, etc.

6. *How do you start your week to maximize your time?*

I start every Monday morning with my plan. This includes what my calendar might look like: what studies do I have coming up? What classes am I teaching? What sermon/s am I working on? Who do I have to call? etc. I then prioritize what needs to be done first. This way I have a plan to meet my deadlines. I always have to leave room for the unexpected. One never knows when a brother or sister will want to talk for a few hours, etc. Always expect the unexpected.

7. *What's the biggest challenge you've faced as a preacher? How did you handle it?*

Like any profession, I have had some challenges. One of the biggest personal challenges was telling a well-intentioned brother that he was not an effective Bible teacher. This is a man who lost his wife, would do anything for anyone, took time off work to comfort those who lost loved ones when he really couldn't afford it, etc. When this same man tried to teach an adult Bible class, it wasn't going well and I was asked to invite him to no longer teach. Other challenges include Christians NOT acting like Christians, including elders, other preachers, etc. This can get nasty at times. Some of my best friends are fellow preachers and elders I have worked with, but certain other preachers/elders make me wonder what their real motive is and keep me wondering, "when will the humility kick in?"

8. *How does your wife help you in your ministry?*

My wife has been a great resource for me in my chosen career! Fortunately, on our first date we covered what we wanted to do with our life: I wanted to preach full time and she wanted to be a stay-at-home wife/mom. We now both do what we want! Most first dates don't work out that well! She has followed me wherever I thought was best for us. She gives input of course! And what input my wife gives, I pay careful attention to. She is one of the smartest people I know. She is not a busybody, not a gossip, but is a quiet encourager. I may not always appreciate how tough preachers' wives (and kids) have it. We just try to be ourselves and our house is always open. We have people over 1–2 times per week on average. They may see our house lived in but they see us! We are a family. There is no priestly/laity system where I am located! This invites a relationship and makes it easier to chat about serious things later on.

9. *How do you go about writing a sermon? Topic? Length?*

I think the best way to go about putting a sermon together is simply reading the text. Get a few copies of the Bible and read each translation. Then simply write out your observations including questions and comments. I immerse myself in the selected text for my upcoming sermon and read it daily (even if I think I have it memorized already). The focus always, always, always has to be the Word of God. I always make sure the Bible text is first, and then an illustration of the principle, and then always end with an application. A word of caution here: make sure the illustration you use isn't too cute where your audience forgets the actual meaning or text involved. What do you want your audience to take away?

When teaching a Bible class, I highly suggest reading the book of the Bible that you are teaching at least once a week.

I have a very long list of sermon ideas and topics. I usually have about 3–4 months' worth of outlines in my files nearly ready to go. I dig them out and polish them and then place them at the bottom of the pile. Where do I get all of these ideas? I read! I read the Old Testament for about an hour nearly every day. I then read the New Testament for about an hour nearly every day. I outline each book of the Bible, which takes me a few years. When I am done, I buy a new Bible and start over. When I come across a sermon idea I write it down and keep a file of my ideas to go back later and dive in deeper.

Reading commentaries can be helpful, but only *after* you have immersed yourself in the Word and jotted down your own observations first! Finally, read the Bible regularly. One can read the Bible looking for sermon and class ideas. But you need to read for personal enrichment.

10. *What book have you gifted the most to people?*

I always keep copies of the Bible close by, ready to distribute. Inexpensive copies are easy to obtain. Another book that I find myself buying and giving away is *Invitation to a Spiritual Revolution* by Paul Earnhart. Brother Earnhart gets to the key message of the Sermon on the Mount and underscores our need to be right with God, including checking our motives as to why we do anything. I often buy a copy for new converts to help establish their faith. I will buy copies for high school and college graduates and encourage them to read. I still enjoy reading this book.

11. *What are some of your favorite books to read?*

I like to read *Old Testament Survey* by Wilber Fields. I read this book once a year, which has helped me memorize the Old Testament. Of course, I suggest reading the Bible and outlining each book.

Another book is *Will the Real Heretics Please Stand Up* by David Bercot. This validates what we often teach regarding New Testament Christianity. David Bercot looks at the second and third generation Christians in the early 100s and shares with us his investigation about what the early Christians taught and how they worshipped. This can be eye opening to one who comes out of a denominational background.

I also like to read Wilber Smith's *An Old Testament History: An Overview of Sacred History and Truth*. There are plenty of good Old Testament survey books available. This is my favorite! I read it about once a year and it helps me place the stories of the Old Testament in chronological order. I feel like I have the major stories, people, and events of the Old Testament memorized. Plus, there are plenty of good maps and charts that enhance your study and understanding of the Bible including types and shadows.

12. *When do you know when it's time to move to another work?*

In my 20 years of preaching, I have worked with four different congregations. Those moves were my choice except for one. The question each preacher must ask himself is "am I effective" here at this work?

13. *What advice would you give to other preachers when it comes to work/family balance?*

It is easy to fall into the trap of wanting to go out and save the world and then overlook some of the best prospects you have which are your children in your house. Awareness of this dynamic is much of the battle for many are just oblivious to this fact. Like anything, you have to have balance. Make routines that force family time. Regularly eating meals together, regularly taking trips together, regular home Bible studies together, etc. These will help. I take my kids with me on gospel meetings so they can see what I do. I take them to my office so they can study when I study (our children are homeschooled). When I visit members from the congregation, I take my children with me (as well as other children from the congregation). We share with our kids the major decisions we make in our lives and explain how those are based on God's word.

14. *Timothy had Paul as a mentor. Who was or is your Paul in the faith? In what ways were they able to help you?*

I am blessed to have several mentors available to me. The first being Bill Moseley, who first grabbed onto me when I walked in off the street into a church building. He was preaching then at the Folsom church of Christ (Folsom, CA) and he patiently answered all of my questions by humbly pointing to the word of God and not offering his opinion. That was a great example! I have leaned on him and his godly wife, Willene, for years! They have been spiritual parents to me.

A second mentor is David Posey, who currently preaches for the Folsom church of Christ. David arrived at Folsom shortly after my conversion and I leaned on him hard for my first six years of being a Christian. I would often visit with David at his house, and he has been a great example to me on what it means to be a preacher. David taught me many lessons but mostly to stay local; in other words, stay focused on your local work!

A third mentor is Doy Moyer my uncle! Okay, he's my wife's uncle but I married into the family. I have stayed at Doy's house countless times, and he has always been a source of encouragement to me and my preaching career. I can call on Doy anytime and randomly ask a Bible question and get a 30-minute sermon answer that is just brilliant.

A fourth and final mentor I will mention is Hugh Delong. Hugh was the preacher at the Country Club Road church of Christ (Tucson, AZ) when I entered a preacher-training program there from 1999–2001. Hugh challenged me in ways I never knew I could be challenged. He took me and tailored the program to fit my strengths and weaknesses. He had me outline each book of the Bible during my time. He gave me the ideas about how to study and gave me book suggestions to read. I still call on Hugh more than anyone else since we have a great father/son relationship. I can call Hugh at anytime, and he always makes time for me and has a great Bible answer to my questions. My final project before going off on my own was to teach Romans where Hugh was the only audience member. He threw me numerous curve ball questions that was extremely helpful!

15. *What piece of advice would you give when it comes to evangelism?*

I have some strong opinions about evangelism. This is something I overlooked early in my preaching career. It is way too easy to sit in a study and get acquainted with God's Word and then overlook going out to save souls. Most would agree that evangelism is often overlooked. Since my awakening about this topic, I have written down just about every question I have ever received in a personal Bible study and then used those for Bible classes. Be sure you always pray for opportunities.

Also, we can place ourselves around brethren whom we like and all of the sudden we are in a bubble and have a hard time relating to the common man. I challenge every preacher I know to get out of your office, out of your comfort zone, at least once/week and just talk to people and get to know them. I am currently involved in Toastmasters. My kids keep me busy with coaching sports teams. In the past, I have been a docent at museums, volunteered to work local elections, etc. Just do something to talk to people, otherwise you have an unrealistic approach in applying the Scriptures, in my opinion. We home school our children. The danger of homeschooling can be growing up in a bubble. I have told young men who want to go into preaching (often from homeschool backgrounds who have not interacted with the public) to get a job at McDonalds (any fast food) for six months and that will teach them all they probably need to know about service to others and how the real world operates. Even homeschoolers have opportunities open up to them. We are part of a co-op that includes nearly 200 people and we are part of the leadership. When we meet (once a week), I have been asked to lead everyone in a devotion and prayer. Again, pray for opportunities.

Be careful how you use social media. Like anything, it can be useful or abused. Remember what your purpose is! Are you trying to win political arguments? Score points? Make exclamation points to make yourself feel good? Or are you trying to share the gospel in a spirit of truth and love (Ephesians 4:15)? The gospel is offensive enough and doesn't need us (Christians) being jerks about our presentation. One sister wrote to me privately, "Jeff, the Bible clearly tells us not to get involved in worthless arguments that don't produce anything righteous." What a great reminder by a dear sister who was concerned for me and my abilities. I may persuade someone to agree with me on political and/or social issues, but so what? We need to concern ourselves with bringing people closer to God, or presenting His Truths in a darkened and chaotic world. I post a daily Bible verse with comments and try to make it a quick read.

One final piece of advice I would offer is to make friends with other preachers you respect. Take time to travel to spend time with them. Save time/money to go visit them for a few days. Ask other preachers what they are doing for their current studies, what they are doing evangelistically, and take notes. What works at one place may not work at another location but these exercises prime the pump for new ideas.

16. *How do you decide how many meetings to hold? When should you decline invitations? How do you go about declining invitations?*

One year I held 13 gospel meetings, which was WAY too much! Today I question the reasons for having gospel meetings. Sometimes there can be good reasons to hold one. I like to invite someone I know who has a specialty and let them speak on that. I have seen in the past where a man is brought in and a congregation pays them a lot of money, which they can barely afford, and they consider that's enough for evangelism. Realistically, the local preacher should be out doing this! I have actually held meetings where I have been located. Since I know people in the community, why not have a weekend meeting at your home location dedicated to a theme: evidences, the real Jesus, family, etc.? This gives you an excuse to advertise even more. I now hold 1–2 meetings per year with a focus of going to Romania every 2 years.

The first time Jeff stepped into a church building was during his senior year of college. After growing up a surfer in Southern California, and while earning a degree in history from CSU Sacramento, Jeff Carr became a Christian in 1994. He started preaching full-time in 1999. He and his wife, Jana, then moved to Tucson, AZ, to participate in their preacher-training program. After that, he worked with churches in Louisiana, Texas, and Georgia. He and his family (three children: Lydia age 12, Josiah age 9, Jeremiah age 7) moved to Vancouver, WA, in 2014 and have worked with the Hockinson church of Christ since then. Jeff has held gospel meetings in over 20 states and has preached in five different countries, including in Romania five different times. Jeff publishes a daily Bible verse with comments on email and social media that reaches thousands every day.

Caleb Churchill

1. *How and when did you decide to get into preaching full time? What was your motivation or your WHY?*

I actually never really decided to get into preaching full time. I first came to NYC in summer 2006 to help a new Christian (who I had met in college) teach his friends about Jesus. We worked for the next few summers without pay in the Bronx teaching young people. With each visit, I became more impressed with the incredible need for more evangelists, teachers, and ministers in NYC. When I finished school, I applied to Teach for America hoping they would send me to teach in NYC so I could continue to contribute to the work in the city. Instead they sent me to work in southwest rural Alabama. I loved my time there. But after completing my two-year commitment teaching school in Alabama, I felt the need in NYC was too great and the time was right to move to NYC (since I was only 25 and single at the time). So I gave up my teaching job in Alabama and moved to NYC in August 2012. When I arrived, an opportunity came up for me to begin devoting myself fully to the work of sharing the gospel. Soon after I moved, I began working alongside three other evangelists and a new church was planted on the westside of Harlem.

2. *As a preacher, have you always worked in a full-time setting capacity or have you been like Paul building tents from time to time?*

I am a school teacher by trade. I started teaching 7–12th grade social studies in Alabama and taught for two years before moving to NYC where I have now worked for the past six years as an evangelist.

3. *What one piece of advice would you give a young man who has begun to preach?*

Never forget that "Apart from God you can do nothing." Unless the Lord builds the house, those who labor, labor in vain. Pray early and often every day.

4. *What wisdom would you give a young man who was thinking about getting into preaching? How can one know when to pull the plug with their decision?*

   What we really need, more than professional preachers, is devoted disciples. My advice to any young man with a desire to preach is to simply serve the Lord in whatever you do. Learn a trade that can support your family while trying to please the Lord. Train yourself to work so that you will not be dependent on the gospel to provide for your family. Then if opportunity arises for you to devote yourself fully to the work of the gospel, take advantage of it. Focus on learning to please the Lord and let the Lord open the doors to use you however He sees fit.

5. *How do you start your mornings to maximize your day?*

   On my best days, I begin in the psalms. I start by reading the word. My focus is not on the quantity of reading, but on the quality. After reading, I transition to meditation where I consider how what I have read needs to affect the way that I am living. My time in meditation leads me to prayer as I am inspired with many reasons to praise and adore God, sins to confess, reasons to give thanks, and prayers to request.

6. *How do you start your week to maximize your time?*

   With the Lord's people on the Lord's day. I try to get up very early in the morning on Sundays to have some time alone with God before being with His people. This helps me be prepared to worship, to speak the truth in love, and to provoke my brothers and sisters to love and good deeds.

7. *What's the biggest challenge you've faced as a preacher? How did you handle it?*

   Soon after I began working full-time as an evangelist, I was faced with a crisis in the church I was a part of. There were a few men in this church who were deliberately refusing to obey the scriptures and insisting on their own way who were leading the church astray. After seeking much counsel and praying about the matter, I decided along with three other respected co-workers to leave the group and start a new work in a new neighborhood in NYC. It is a decision we have never regretted, as a healthy diverse church was formed that is still growing steadily and has enjoyed peace and unity since its beginning.

8. *How does your wife help you in your ministry?*

In every way. She is hospitable, opening our home and her life to strangers and to brethren every week. She is working hard daily to teach our children about God and train them up in the way they should go. She counsels younger women who are serving the Lord and teaches children in the church.

9. *How do you go about writing a sermon? Topic? Length?*

Topic: We try to meet with the preachers each year and map a plan for preaching and teaching for the year. At that meeting, we discuss how the church is doing—Where are we strongest? Where are we weakest? We try to plan topics that need to be covered that year. Then we leave space in every month to address problems and issues that may arise. Our planning is always flexible, but it helps to have a plan. We also track our sermons so that we know who spoke, what was the topic, and what texts were discussed. We use these data to help us see what we are focusing on the most and what we are overlooking.

Length: I try to not preach the same amount of time every week. Some are shorter, some are longer, but I try to concern myself more with content and being concise than with length.

Writing: I try to find a quiet place and remove all distractions. Then I write. It's best to write early enough to have a couple days to review it. In my best sermons, I take time to think about what is in this for every member before preaching it. It is my aim to make sure there is something in every sermon for everyone present.

10. *What book have you gifted the most to people?*

For seekers: *Diligently Seeking God.*

For preachers and young men: *Humility—True Greatness* by C.J. Mahaney or *Finally Free* by Heath Lambert.

11. *What are some of your favorite books to read?*

I like to read the scriptures and books that were written around the same time scripture was written. I enjoy the writings of early Christians. I enjoy reading C.S. Lewis, as well as other great Christian thinkers. I enjoy reading Tim Keller because he has worked as a pastor in NYC for 30 years. I enjoy reading about marriage, the evidence for the resurrection, and the perspectives of others on the gospel and the scriptures.

12. *When do you know when it's time to move to another work?*

I'm pretty young so I've only done this once. My rule was "when I've worked myself out of job"—when I've trained enough others to do what I am doing so that the work can continue in my absence, then it is time to move on.

13. *What advice would you give to other preachers when it comes to work/family balance?*

Your work as a minister can become an idol. For this reason, it is vital that you set aside holy time for the Lord and for family. I take one day a week where I do not work; that day is completely devoted to taking care of my family and spending time with them. I try to set aside daily time for me to be in the word only for myself—not to teach, but to learn.

There is a temptation for preachers to become lazy since there is often far less accountability. You ought to be working longer than the average working man in your community since you are working for the Lord. The average Christian man works to support his family *and* works to contribute to the work of the gospel. I try to think about the time that my brothers are working plus the time that they are putting into helping the church and I want to be working at least that long.

14. *Timothy had Paul as a mentor. Who was or is your Paul in the faith? In what ways were they able to help you?*

When I was in high school, Gary Fisher took me aside and taught me the gospel of Mark and then showed me how to share it with others. From that time on, he has been a close mentor in my life who I go to often for counsel. Soon after I started going to Sewell Hall and Paul Earnhart's camp in Alabama. Both Sewell and Paul became two men I often turn to always for advice on any important decision. To this day, I still turn to them for counsel and wisdom, especially when making big decisions. These men have taught me how to do the work of an evangelist and how to grow as a husband and a father.

15. *What piece of advice would you give when it comes to evangelism?*

Jesus tells us to **go** make disciples. Whatever you do, don't wait for people to come to you. It is your responsibility to take the gospel to the people. It is our privilege to preach to those who want to hear and even to those who do not, just as the great prophets of old also did.

16. *How do you decide how many meetings to hold? When should you decline invitations? How do you go about declining invitations?*

Deciding how many: I make every effort to not be gone more than a month at most. It is hard to be effective in my work if I'm gone more than a month of the year. Some years I need to be gone less for family reasons. I don't have a set number that I do, rather I consider the need in every opportunity and my usefulness in fulfilling the need and make a decision after considering and discussing with my wife.

How to decide: Questions to consider:

- Have I been away from my family too much? Can I take my family with me?
- Have I been away from the church too much? Will it be helpful or harmful for me to be gone?
- Will this church be able to find someone else who will be able to fill this need?
- Could someone else do this just as well as I can?
- Will this open up more doors of opportunity to spread the gospel?

When to Decline: If I have already reached a month of travel for the year, I will decline. Also, if I feel there is no real need for me, I will often decline. Sometimes I will accept though if there is an opportunity for me to grow from accepting.

How to Decline: I think the easiest way is to say "I'm sorry, I'm not going to be able to do it." Sometimes, I will offer to do something in the future instead.

Caleb Churchill grew up in Indiana, but after finishing school in Florida and Kentucky, he began working as a teacher at Marengo High School in south Alabama in 2010 through a program called Teach For America. After two years of teaching in the classroom, he moved to New York City and began devoting himself fully to teaching the gospel. While living in the Bronx for five years, he married Lindsey, the love of his life, and helped to plant the West Harlem Church in Upper Manhattan. Caleb and Lindsey have two sons together, Cyrus and Cyprian. In late 2017, Caleb and his family moved to Flatbush in Brooklyn where they began working with a group of disciples to spread the gospel across the borough. To learn more about this work in Brooklyn, you can visit www.thewaybk.com. Caleb has been blessed with opportunities to preach and teach in the Caribbean, Latin America, and in Africa. He enjoys traveling and meeting God's people from all over the globe.

Brady Cook

1. *How and when did you decide to get into preaching full time? What was your motivation or your WHY?*

My journey into preaching started in April 2006. I remember hearing another young preacher give a sermon at a small congregation outside of Nacogdoches, TX, and thought to myself, "I could do that." While that initial motivation may be less-than-stellar, it quickly became something that I get to do instead of something that I had to do. We only have a short amount of time on this earth, and I plan on spending it working toward something that's eternal, in whatever capacity I can.

2. *As a preacher, have you always worked in a full-time setting capacity or have you been like Paul building tents from time to time?*

The first two years that I did freelance preaching, I worked a few odd jobs since I was also in school at the time. Mostly running a paper route (which is surprisingly a fantastic job for a college kid) and working at the university recreation center. The last two years I was in school were spent in a preacher-training program, where I also spent Sunday mornings preaching at a small congregation just outside of Lufkin, TX. This not only helped supplement my income, but also provided invaluable experience putting together classes and sermons on a regular basis. Since leaving school and moving to Greenville, TX, I have been (very) fortunate to be fully supported by Hillside.

3. *What one piece of advice would you give a young man who has begun to preach?*

I'm sure I'm not old enough to really be dispensing that much advice, but one thing I have always heard, and still rings true today, is "Don't preach because you can, preach because you can't do anything else." Translation: Preach because your soul demands you preach, instead of simply looking at it as another vocation. Also, spend the first few years (and the next 100 after that, actually) grounded firmly in Bible study. Public speaking, classroom management, organizational skills, all of that will come with time. First things first.

4. *What wisdom would you give a young man who was thinking about getting into preaching? How can one know when to pull the plug with their decision?*

I was fortunate enough to move directly from school to preaching, but I know of several who have had to break away from their secular jobs to make that transition, and sometimes with a family in tow. The switch is hard and can come with some hesitation, but I would say to start small, filling in from time to time, and then make the jump if the opportunity presents itself. I have no doubt that anyone can become a preacher, but I've seen a few people leave the secular world and get into preaching, only to enter a bad situation, get soured, and leave the work entirely. Everyone has to be on board—wife, kids, support system, etc.—or else your work will absolutely be affected.

5. *How do you start your mornings to maximize your day?*

I like getting up early (although with two kids under the age of 3, it's tougher than it used to be), but there's nothing better than working out and getting 15 minutes of alone time with God while the world is still dark. Whether that's prayer, Bible reading, or both, my mind has to be centered on what's important before I make any kind of reasonable progress. Get some face time in with the members too, if you can. There's a group of men from the church here who eat breakfast together every morning, so I try to make it there once or twice a week. Not only does that help me feel like part of a community, but it reminds me that the people I preach to are real human beings with real lives that need real spiritual teaching.

6. *How do you start your week to maximize your time?*

Hit the ground running. I know most preachers like to take Mondays off, but my brain doesn't work like that. I can't relax until the more visual things are taken care of: class, sermons, articles, etc. Then I backfill my week with seeing members, going into the community, and studies. Works better for me that way, but everyone is different. Also, I'm a big fan of to-do lists. I'm a visual person, so it helps me to see it all laid out.

7. *What's the biggest challenge you've faced as a preacher? How did you handle it?*

I've always struggled with anxiety and depression, and that was more pronounced once I started preaching. For that reason, I really grapple with imposter syndrome, or feeling like I don't belong in the pulpit. Having close preacher friends and a super supportive congregation helps, but it ultimately comes back to reminding myself that I am the messenger and He is the message. It's not now, nor has it ever been, about me, and I try to remind myself of that daily.

8. *How does your wife help you in your ministry?*

Next to the Bible, a good wife is the most important piece in the preaching puzzle. She is my best encouragement when I'm down, and my strongest critic when I need to improve. She can read me like no one else can, suggest ways for the work to improve, and takes the initiative to make the people from Hillside feel special. To her credit, she has never once resented being a preacher's wife, nor complained about the adjustments that such a lifestyle puts on our family. I look up to her more than she will ever know; I can't imagine going through the things we've gone through without her.

9. *How do you go about writing a sermon? Topic? Length?*

Since we only have Sunday mornings, I have 13 topics that I rotate through every quarter: exhortation, expository, kingdom, doctrinal, first principles, evangelism, young people, minor prophets, Bible study, world events, Jesus, character study, and oddball (random sermon that doesn't fit into another category). These will inevitably overlap (i.e., there's obviously more than one doctrinal type sermon every quarter), and I try to think about what our congregation needs specifically in this quarter to fill those topics. I start researching a sermon loosely about six weeks in advance of the time, then write the sermon based on that research the week of. I use an outline that's normally 3–4 pages that ends up being 35–40 minutes.

10. *What book have you gifted the most to people?*

This is subject to change almost by the month, but the book I've recommended lately is *Screwtape Letters* by C.S. Lewis. Not only did that book help me consider just how prevalent sin is in our lives, but it also challenged my worldview (in a good way). Doctrinally speaking, the book I've recommend *is Old Light on New Worship* by John Price, which discusses the scriptural argument against instrumental music in a very detailed way. Secularly, one of my all-time favorites is *The Sunflower* by Simon Wiesenthal. If you haven't read it, do yourself a favor and pick it up.

11. *What are some of your favorite books to read?*

History, history, history. I'm not much into the fluffy contemporary religious books, but anything with substance that can provide context to events that we're already familiar with are always welcome on my shelf. I'm also trying really hard to get into reading fiction, but it's just not working for me...yet.

12. *When do you know when it's time to move to another work?*

I'm still at my first full-time work so I'm not very qualified to speak on this subject, but provided that you and your current work are still working well together, you should consider leaving if you better feel you can serve the kingdom elsewhere. Money is never a good reason to leave, nor is personal glory. It doesn't matter the size of the church you're moving to, it matters how effectively you think you can build up the local work there. If that's greater than where you're at, it might be time to make a move.

13. *What advice would you give to other preachers when it comes to work/family balance?*

I'll never forget a story Warren Berkley told me once. After a meeting, when an older preacher noticed Warren bringing his briefcase home with him to work on the weekend, the older preacher gently took the briefcase, put it in the foyer, and said, "Leave that here." As preachers, we're never off-duty, but sometimes the best thing we can do for the kingdom is to be with our families, both to help them and for our own personal sanity.

Too many preachers have made wrecks of their lives by focusing on everyone else's lives but their own family, and the result was catastrophic. When it comes to striking a strong work-life balance, be intentional about it. Set a schedule, make allowances when you can, but remember your place as head of the household.

14. *Timothy had Paul as a mentor. Who was or is your Paul in the faith? In what ways were they able to help you?*

There are a couple people who could fit this description, but to me, there's only one that matches it perfectly: Jim McDonald. He trained me and another young preacher for two years, listened to countless awful sermons from me, labored through classes where I just couldn't grasp the material, and then, when I was finished with the two years, recommended me for the work in Greenville. Though I haven't been in the training program for nearly a decade, he still calls regularly just to check up on me, which usually results in an hour-long phone call, at least. I will forever be indebted to him not only for his counsel and example, but for his love and patience with a young preacher. I love you, papa.

15. *What piece of advice would you give when it comes to evangelism?*

People have different systems to help spread the Word, from flip charts to visitor follow-up programs, but in my opinion, evangelism flows best when it flows through relationships. I also believe that no one person at the church should be the only one evangelizing, but as Paul told Timothy, part of our role as preachers is to "equip the saints for ministry" (Ephesians 4:12). We tend to be isolated as preachers, staying inside our office and afraid to venture into the big, scary world, but we have to take the Word to the streets. Get involved in the community, spend time getting to know your neighbors, volunteer at your local hospital, bring up God in everyday conversation, and most importantly, pray for opportunities, and doors will begin to open.

16. *How do you decide how many meetings to hold? When should you decline invitations? How do you go about declining invitations?*

When I first started doing meetings, my elders decided on a set number of weeks I could be gone for both vacation and work-related activities (meetings, lectureships, etc.). So far, that initial criteria haven't changed, and I haven't had to decline very many meetings. The ones that I have declined were normally because of scheduling conflicts.

Brady Cook was born in Amarillo, TX, and earn a BBA from Stephen F. Austin in marketing and an MS in history from Texas A&M University – Commerce. He married to Melina Turnbow and they have two kids: Logan (2) and Hannah (10 months).

Brady trained under Jim McDonald and Kyle Campbell for two years at Loop 287 church of Christ in Lufkin, TX (2007–2009). He has served at Hillside church of Christ since 2009. He runs www.coffeeandaBible.com.

Christopher Eppler

1. *How and when did you decide to get into preaching full time? What was your motivation or your WHY?*

   I was living in the Chattanooga, TN, area prior to getting married. My wife's grandfather was worshipping with a small church in north Georgia at the time. He asked me if I would be willing to do some appointment preaching for them for a little while. This appointment preaching became full-time preaching. My father was a full-time preacher from the time I was 12 years old. I never really considered following in his steps, but that is exactly what ended up happening! The more I preached, the more I loved doing it. It is truly a wonderful blessing to be there at the moment that someone decides to follow Jesus or to see a light go off as someone understands something from the Word that they previously did not understand.

2. *As a preacher, have you always worked in a full-time setting capacity or have you been like Paul building tents from time to time?*

   I have worked solely as an evangelist for most of the time I have been preaching. There were a few years at my second work when I did not have enough outside support and spent some time sitting with the elderly and working at a Western Auto to provide additional income. Having a job in addition to preaching certainly brings its challenges and I have a great appreciation for those that do such.

3. *What one piece of advice would you give a young man who has begun to preach?*

   Surround yourself with wise men. As a young man, we simply do not have the ability yet to carefully think through a situation and separate the emotion out from it. The tendency of the young man will be to overreact and make a mess of the situation. However, if that same young man has a group of wise men to lean on and the wisdom to not make a difficult decision until speaking with those wise men, he will do amazingly better. This can be a difficult thing to accomplish because often times young preachers are in small, remote locations away from other preachers. The effort may be greater for that young man to have a group of wise men that he can call up, but its value is far above the extra effort he may have to put in.

4. *What wisdom would you give a young man who was thinking about getting into preaching? How can one know when to pull the plug with their decision?*

Get some training. I went to the school of hard-knocks. While that is valuable in many ways, it also can be a hindrance. Spending time with an older preacher who is good at delivering lessons and learning from him is huge. You will be far more effective than trying to figure it out on your own by mimicking what you think you have heard other preachers do. Spending time with an older preacher who is effective at teaching the lost is huge. Many times, young preachers are not teaching the lost simply because they have no clue how to get started doing it. If we are not careful, that ignorance can carry on for years and the work will suffer as a result. I never really figured my work out until I had the good fortune of living around a great personal worker, Don Swanson, and a couple excellent presenters, Max Dawson and David Banning.

Preachers are not constantly on cloud nine about preaching! Some days we may be feeling it and others not so much. And that is okay. However, if I have been pursuing preaching for a time and cannot seem to get excited about doing it, there may be a bigger problem there. Often one finds out after getting into it that it is not what they thought it was. The work is not so much about making and presenting a sermon, but is about people. If at that point you are not in love with the idea of navigating people, then it is time to do something else. That is okay. Paul was under obligation to preach (Romans 1:14), we are not. If we decide that it is not for us, we can move on and do something else without condemnation.

5. *How do you start your mornings to maximize your day?*

I like to start my mornings by doing some reading. I read my Bible. I read a spiritual article or two that helps me think about something spiritual in depth. After I am done reading, I like to do a few tasks on my to-do list for the day that I can quickly complete. This gets the ball rolling for me to accomplish greater tasks as the day unfolds.

6. *How do you start your week to maximize your time?*

I begin my week on Monday. Early on I took Mondays off, but I finally decided that this was a mistake. When I took Mondays off, it always felt like the week got a slow start. Like I was a day behind everyone else. Now I begin my week on Monday at the office. I try to begin on Monday doing some simple tasks that I can easily knock out that helps me feel like I am accomplishing something from the beginning.

7. *What's the biggest challenge you've faced as a preacher? How did you handle it?*

Helping the church to get properly organized. Many of the Lord's churches are organized properly in position only, but not in substance. There are shepherds and deacons, but they are not doing what the New Testament defines their jobs to be. Through great effort, patience, study, and mentoring, we have been able to find the way forward to proper organization. It required years of effort, but the fruit finally began to come in and has been phenomenal.

As a young preacher I had never thought about proper organization and had no clue how to begin. My first step was to find some preachers who had studied this issue thoroughly and learn from them. The instruction from these men was invaluable. I then sat down with the shepherds and we began a plan for moving forward. It could take years and likely will be a labor that extends beyond my tenure.

8. *How does your wife help you in your ministry?*

The biggest help my wife has been comes from her calm demeanor. It is hard to get her riled up, and this complements my high-strung nature very well. Although I may not always appreciate it in the moment, her calm words to help me think things through have been invaluable to me.

Even when things are not going well, Molly has a smile on her face. She is always kind. She has a way of saying difficult things to people in a way that they can accept. This quiet grace has proved to be an enormous help, not only to myself, but also to the good brethren that we worship with.

9. *How do you go about writing a sermon? Topic? Length?*

I tend to do a basic three- or four-point outline. My preference is to teach from a single text and make the points that the author makes from that text. Even when I preach on a topic, I prefer to simply go to a place where that topic is addressed and make the points from that text that the author makes on that topic. My goal is for my sermons to be about 30 minutes in length.

I took the advice of Mark Roberts and Warren Berkley years ago and began planning my sermons a quarter at a time. Sometimes that schedule gets messed up, but it is at least a plan in place that does away with the weekly fear of what I will preach on Sunday! Thus I have my main idea and main text already plotted out. Then I begin researching that text and outline the points made by the author.

10. *What book have you gifted the most to people?*

There are two books that I give to people regularly. The first is *Will the Real Heretics Please Stand Up* by David Bercot. The early church writers offer so much in way of support for the restoration plea. We can read their writings and see that just as we see in the New Testament, so did the early saints for the few centuries following the close of the New Testament era. Bercot's book concisely summarizes these writings for us in such a way that it is a real faith booster, as we see the early saints doing and believing as we do today.

The second book that I give out with probably equal frequency is Dave Ramsey's *Total Money Makeover*. I give a copy of this book to every couple that I counsel, especially for pre-marital counseling. The issue of finance in the home is such a problem for the majority of Americans. If couples will read this book and put the principles into effect, much misery can be avoided.

11. *What are some of your favorite books to read?*

I enjoy reading books about the ante-Nicene writers immensely. I find the writings of these individuals to be faith-building as I see how they dealt with the various problems they faced, inclusive of the persecution they endured. I also enjoy reading books about evangelism and organization, such as the various books put out by Rainer.

12. *When do you know when it's time to move to another work?*

This can be a very difficult question to answer. My standard has generally been to examine myself periodically and determine if I am being effective. I only intend on remaining at a place as long as I am effective. Am I being heard? Are people putting into action what I speak? Are people being won to the gospel through my efforts? I ask myself questions like these to determine where I stand.

Sometimes a preacher asks themselves this question because the work is not at peace. There will always be battles to be fought and just because I am involved in a battle does not mean that it is time to go. The church needs men that will stand up and fight a necessary battle. However, there is also a point where the church is just not at peace and I may well not be the right man for the job. It is easy as a preacher to feel that the entire work depends on me remaining and doing what I do. But I have found that this is rarely, if ever, the case. Preachers depart and works carry on, even troubled works.

I try to periodically self-evaluate while at the same time realizing that the work pre-existed me and will be after my departure also. My job is to advance the work along as far as I can for the time that I am here.

13. *What advice would you give to other preachers when it comes to work/family balance?*

Work hard, but do not neglect family. Too many preachers win the lost and lose their families! What have I accomplished when I do such? We need to be responsible and put in a full week's work just like any other person, but we must also unplug from work and spend time with our families just like other people do also. That means not bringing home a pile of work. That means not staying on the phone constantly dealing with brotherhood issues while at home. That means taking real vacations where the church is left to those at home while you are away. That means spending quality time with your wife.

As a young preacher, it is important to remember that the work was there before you and will carry on after. Everything does not rise and fall on you. Put in your time as a worker, but put in your time as a father and husband also. It is easy to get caught in the trap of feeling like everything related to church is your job, but it is not. Allow others the opportunity to step up so you will not become overburdened and hinder the church in doing so.

14. *Timothy had Paul as a mentor. Who was or is your Paul in the faith? In what ways were they able to help you?*

I grew up worshipping at the Milam Street church in Jasper, TX. Our preacher for those first 10 years or so was brother Jim McDonald. I learned much of what I know biblically from his training. He taught my father the gospel when I was six and is largely responsible for my family serving Christ to this day. In my adult life, I have been blessed to spend a good deal of time learning further from brother Jim and have even traveled with him to the Philippines on two different occasions. His wisdom and work ethic have been an inspiration to me.

I have been doubly blessed by a second mentor and advisor that came from the same source. After Jim McDonald left the work at Jasper in 1990, brother Shane Carrington moved to work there. Shane seemed old at the time (I was 10), but in reality, he was only about 23 years old. Many hours were spent at Shane and Kelly's house over those years, and as an adult Shane has been an invaluable advisor and confidant. Shane has always been my slightly older, cool head source. When youth has interfered with my decision making, Shane has been like an older, wiser brother who has helped me reason through things calmly to make better decisions.

15. *What piece of advice would you give when it comes to evangelism?*

Do it. It is so daunting when starting a new work as a young preacher. We can easily become consumed by trying to keep our head above water, preaching two sermons and teaching some Bible classes. Yet, that pulpit work is just a fraction of what we do. The real work that an evangelist does happens in the streets, at the post office, the grocery store, and in people's homes. The evangelist must be busy teaching the gospel to the lost. It is an art. The best thing that a young man can do is find an older preacher that is good at teaching the lost and learn that art.

16. *How do you decide how many meetings to hold? When should you decline invitations? How do you go about declining invitations?*

I have never been one to do many meetings. Generally speaking my invitations to speak have been within the guidelines of what the shepherds have allotted for me to be away. My rule has simply been that I will not allow the work at home to suffer to preach elsewhere. I would not accept an invitation that would hinder something important at home or that would not allow me the time to properly do the work at home. On the rare occasion where I have had to decline an invitation, I have found that gently explaining the situation has been warmly accepted by the brethren making the request.

Christopher Eppler is 37 years old and has worked for the church in Mauriceville, TX, for the past 10 years. Prior to this work, he worked with the church in Corrigan, TX, and the church in Rock Spring, GA. He is the husband of Molly and has three children.

Ryan Goodwin

1. *How and when did you decide to get into preaching full time? What was your motivation or your WHY?*

I began offering short invitations as a teenager while I was a member of the Beaverton church of Christ in my hometown of Beaverton, OR. I've always been comfortable in front of crowds, so serving publicly was no problem. However, I was determined to follow a musical career after high school, studying as a music major at the University of Oregon. It was in Eugene that I had a chance to present my first full-length sermon. I guess a passion was awakened and I resolved to transfer schools, find a preacher training program somewhere, and make preaching my life. Music felt like a hobby, while preaching felt like a purpose.

2. *As a preacher, have you always worked in a full-time setting capacity or have you been like Paul building tents from time to time?*

Once the decision was made to change my educational trajectory, I was all in with preaching. I never had a plan B if preaching didn't work out. Fortunately, I've always worked with churches that were financially capable of supporting me with a living wage.

3. *What one piece of advice would you give a young man who has begun to preach?*

Expect a lot from yourself. Set the bar high when it comes to moral behavior, how you express your love, your work ethic, your willingness to try new things, and stretch yourself. Believe that you can achieve great things with the help of loving elders, mentors, a supportive family, and most of all, God (who is the One who gives us our talents to begin with).

4. *What wisdom would you give a young man who was thinking about getting into preaching? How can one know when to pull the plug with their decision?*

Many have said it before, but it's worth repeating: If there is anything else you *can* do and still feel spiritually enriched and satisfied, then do it. The world needs preachers, but it also needs

Christian craftsmen, businessmen, teachers, and community leaders whose influence can help open doors for the gospel. You will know full-time, professional preaching isn't for you when you start making excuses for poor performance, when you resent church members for asking a lot from you, when you become jealous of the success of other preachers, or when you've become apathetic to your own expectations.

5. *How do you start your mornings to maximize your day?*

I get up with my kids and get them ready for school. I put a premium on being the last person my children see before walking into the school yard. I never leave the house before I've seen all of my children.

6. *How do you start your week to maximize your time?*

Some preachers thrive in a rigid, structured work environment. Others, like me, thrive when there is some (not too much, of course) totally unstructured time built into the weekly schedule. Some of my best brainstorming happens when I get to the office and just take time to meditate, read, relax my brain, and listen to music. Sundays are mentally and physically exhausting for me because I'm an energetic, physical, enthusiastic preacher. I need quiet time in my office to re-charge and let new, fresh ideas comes to me organically. Maybe other preachers are different, but I'm not capable of manufacturing creativity or forcing myself to come up with sermon ideas. The best ideas come as a result of studying, of course, but some of my best studying happens when I'm allowed to explore the Word without schedule constraints.

7. *What's the biggest challenge you've faced as a preacher? How did you handle it?*

Figuring out where my family's limits are. My wife and children only thrive when I don't run them into the ground with too many social obligations or unrealistic expectations.

8. *How does your wife help you in your ministry?*

She's incredibly supportive of me behind the scenes. She is the only one with whom I share my frustrations. She is an incredibly introverted, private person (my polar opposite), but this disarms me and allows me to be very vulnerable with her. Her introversion feels safe to me—an ideal quality for a confidant.

9. *How do you go about writing a sermon? Topic? Length?*

Most weeks when I'm scheduled to preach two sermons, I use one sermon for a more challenging topic (something doctrinal, explaining a tough text, addressing a specific sin, challenging biases, etc.) and the other for something more uplifting, approachable to a visitor, or more practical. Most sermons take me one or two days to complete. I start with a basic idea, handwrite notes in my sermon journal, read books or article pertinent to the subject, then begin pulling it all together in a PowerPoint file. I do not use notes for my sermons, but go straight from the PowerPoint slides. The finished product is proofread and then allowed to sit for a day or two. I always look over the sermon on Friday after I've slept on it, just to make sure I'm still happy with the work. I keep a log of my sermons to make sure I'm addressing a broad range of topics and balancing topical and textual. Heavy, text-based sermons are important because they show familiarity with the great source material and a commitment to letting the Word speak for itself.

10. *What book have you gifted the most to people?*

I've shared marriage material more than anything else, actually. Dr. Crabb's *The Marriage Builder* is a personal favorite.

11. *What are some of your favorite books to read?*

For pleasure, historical non-fiction (military history, American history, sports history, exploration and adventure-seeking, etc.). For work, the best book I've ever read (and I am continually reading it, it seems) is *The Life and Times of Jesus the Messiah* by Edersheim. It's an exhaustive, sweeping, often heartbreaking look at the cultural, social, political, and religious background of every aspect of Jesus' ministry.

12. *When do you know when it's time to move to another work?*

When the opportunity comes to me and it feels right. I've learned the hard way that it's foolishness to try and fabricate opportunities. Preachers come across as weaselly when they snoop around, ask other preachers to "put in a good word for me," or spend all their time waiting to pounce on a soon-to-be open position somewhere.

As far as my own moves, the first was made because I wanted to go from a church without elders to one with elders. I was young and knew I would develop better as a preacher under Biblical leadership. I stayed with that church six years because of my relationship with the elders. The next move I made was to Arizona, my wife's home state. When a preacher has a chance to move his wife and kids near family, he'd better give that opportunity a long, hard look. Most preachers end up living very far from family, and I'm incredibly blessed that my kids get to be near grandparents. There are many reasons to move from church to another, but the value of family shouldn't be discounted.

13. *What advice would you give to other preachers when it comes to work/family balance?*

Don't let them come into conflict. Don't make your wife resent the elders because you spend more time with them than her. Don't cross any lines when it comes to relationships with female church members. Don't violate your family's privacy (we keep many conversations with church members confident, so give the same privilege to family members). For as much as we need to be available, make sure family time is not being sacrificed. It's okay to leave the phone off. It's okay to go on vacation.

14. *Timothy had Paul as a mentor. Who was or is your Paul in the faith? In what ways were they able to help you?*

My mentor in Little Rock, AR, was Dennis Carrow. My mentor in Beaverton, OR, was Mark Dunagan. We've maintained a close relationship. Both men have always been willing to answer questions, even decades later.

15. *What piece of advice would you give when it comes to evangelism?*

Don't get discouraged. We go through phases in evangelism, where one year might be very fruitful and yield dozens of studies and baptisms, and another year might feel like hitting a brick wall at every turn. It's okay. During the dry spells, turn your attention to more internal matters of the congregation. Preach more on family issues, congregational unity, leadership development, etc. When the evangelism picks back up, go back to the basics, such as salvation, overcoming sin, personal spiritual growth, etc. Make sure your preaching is reflective of the church's needs at that moment, while keeping an eye to the future. You will always be relevant as long as you're keeping your preaching in the Word!

16. *How do you decide how many meetings to hold? When should you decline invitations? How do you go about declining invitations?*

I typically do not have these kinds of problems.

Ryan Goodwin works with the Monte Vista church of Christ, a thriving, diverse congregation near the urban heart of Phoenix, AZ. He is happily married and has three young children. Growing up in Oregon, Ryan began preaching at a very young age and pursued his education at the University of Oregon and Portland State University.

Robert Harkrider

1. *How and when did you decide to get into preaching full time? What was your motivation or your WHY?*

I had just celebrated my sixteenth birthday when I was asked to prepare a sermon and preach for a small country church. Soon after that, two other churches asked me to come, so I developed a routine of preparing a sermon one week and then delivering that lesson the next three Sundays. This opportunity enabled me to gain experience so that I was invited to preach most every Sunday through the rest of high school and through college. By the time, I graduated from college I knew that I wanted to devote my life to preaching in a full-time capacity.

My motivation to preach was no doubt generated by two godly parents who loved the Lord and were faithful to every period of worship. They encouraged me to study the Bible and develop faith at an early age. Often, we had gospel preachers as guests in our home, men whom I learned to admire.

2. *As a preacher, have you always worked in a full-time setting capacity or have you been like Paul building tents from time to time?*

I have always worked in a full-time capacity.

3. *What one piece of advice would you give a young man who has begun to preach?*

The best advice I could give was first given to me by my mother: "Study the Bible; read and pray, then study, study, study!"

4. *What wisdom would you give a young man who was thinking about getting into preaching? How can one know when to pull the plug with their decision?*

The decision to preach must emanate from a heart that is burning to teach lost souls the gospel. One must realize that the work of evangelism is a life and not merely a nine-to-five job. Furthermore, one's conscience needs to be motivated by realizing that "responsibility is measured by ability plus opportunity." Has

God set before me the opportunity? And has He given me the talent (ability)? Is it my responsibility to glorify God by a lifetime of evangelism?

5. *How do you start your mornings to maximize your day?*

Start each morning with prayer. Write down a list of goals to accomplish that day. Then get busy!

6. *How do you start your week to maximize your time?*

Writing a list and determining things of greatest priority is important. There will usually be interruptions (e.g., members with special needs, family concerns), so the list will get altered as the week goes by. Some things will get pushed to the next week, but time set aside for study and sermon preparation must not be neglected by mundane affairs.

7. *What's the biggest challenge you've faced as a preacher? How did you handle it?*

My biggest challenge as a preacher arose when a member of the local congregation began teaching false doctrine. Like 2 Peter 2 and the book of Jude describe, this teacher was at first unsuspected. If left alone, division is certain. A face to face study comes first. If that does not bear success, then take to the elders. If that does not work, then publicly expose the false doctrine, Romans 16:17.

8. *How does your wife help you in your ministry?*

My wife has been a blessing. When the children were young, her major attention was dealing with their daily needs. But she was always supportive and involved in major decisions. After the children were grown, she has been able to spend more time in private teaching. We work together as a team.

9. *How do you go about writing a sermon? Topic? Length?*

Sermon preparation starts by first determining what is needed. What is the motivation for teaching this lesson? This may be determined by different sources: a) a topic needed by the church;

b) personal study of a particular scripture; c) an excellent article; d) request by someone, etc. Its length is basically determined by the nature of its content. Fill the lesson with God's word, not jokes and anecdotes that merely entertain rather than edify. A good rule to follow is to remember that the mind can absorb what the seat can endure, so guard against too much. On the other hand, remember that sermonettes produce only Christianettes!

10. *What book have you gifted the most to people?*

Because I wrote the Truth Publications commentary on *Revelation*, I have gifted that more than any other.

11. *What are some of your favorite books to read?*

My favorite books to read have been the Bible first and then good commentaries that explain the text. When reading other books, choose those written by brethren or at least by conservative scholars, such as Jack Cottrell, Homer Hailey, Paul Butler.

12. *When do you know when it's time to move to another work?*

It is time to move when you have greater opportunity to reach the lost in another place. In other words, it may be best to stay where you are so long as the brethren are being edified and outreach to the lost is accomplished. Pray without ceasing about it. The Lord opens doors when it is time to move, but He closes doors by making difficult any change.

13. *What advice would you give to other preachers when it comes to work/family balance?*

In the words of Homer Hailey, he said, "Do not be so busy trying to save others that you neglect your own children and lose them." Some weeks your full attention is given to the work of evangelism, but other weeks will allow you to set aside special time for wife and children. Keep a balance by proving your love for family.

14. *Timothy had Paul as a mentor. Who was or is your Paul in the faith? In what ways were they able to help you?*

Sewell Hall has to me always been the model of what a gospel preacher should be. His advice and friendship have been of great encouragement. His example in life has demonstrated a total commitment to the Lord, like Paul said, "to whom I belong and whom I serve" (Acts 27:23).

15. *What piece of advice would you give when it comes to evangelism?*

Preach the Word! Learn a good method, or series, to use in private one on one studies. More conversions these days are done through private studies. Gospel meetings are still effective in stirring up faith, edifying the brethren, but conversions of alien sinners are not as prevalent as in former days. So remember that evangelism literally means to bring the good news. Therefore, fill your life with teaching both privately and publicly.

16. *How do you decide how many meetings to hold? When should you decline invitations? How do you go about declining invitations?*

Priority of your time must be given to the local work with which you accepted obligation. The elders should be consulted about the number of weeks one may be away during a year. If invitations exceed the number of weeks agreed upon, then ask the one extending an invitation if the meeting can be scheduled in a later year. Keep good records and ask for a hard copy to keep in your files.

Born February 4, 1939, Robert Fisher Harkrider began studying to preach the gospel while in high school. Upon graduating with a B.S. from Stephen F. Austin University, Robert and his wife, Arline Cope Thorp, moved to work three years each with the churches in Pinson, AL, and Hueytown, AL, and then to Sydney, N.S.W. Australia, for two and a half years. He returned to the United States in 1969 to work five years with the East Florence church in Alabama. In 1974, he moved to Houston, TX, to work with the Spring Branch church. In 1977, he moved to Nacogdoches, the city of his youth, to work nine years with the Mound and Starr congregation. In 1986, he moved to Orlando, FL, and worked with the S. Bumby church 31 years.

Robert has published 30 workbooks that include both topic studies and a mini-commentary on all of the O.T. books of prophecy and all the books of the New Testament. Also, the complete series of Discovering God's Way Bible class literature was developed and edited by Robert and Arline. They are blessed with four children: Beth Creel (Richard); John Thorp; Amy Bruns (Glenn); and Anne Underwood (Tip).

Shawn Jeffries

1. *How and when did you decide to get into preaching full time? What was your motivation or your WHY?*

    I decided that I wanted to preach shortly after I got married when I was 20 years old. At first, all I wanted to do was preach occasionally and work a secular job. After I graduated from college (and once I was blessed to find someone to invest their time in training me), I then got the fire in my belly to devote my life to the work of preaching. There are really two reasons why I decided to become a preacher: I love God and I love people. It is really that simple for me. The day I stop loving those two things, I will stop preaching.

2. *As a preacher, have you always worked in a full-time setting capacity or have you been like Paul building tents from time to time?*

    Since becoming a preacher, I have never worked a secular job. I prefer to never have to. I want to devote all my time and energy to the work of studying and preaching.

3. *What one piece of advice would you give a young man who has begun to preach?*

    The piece of advice I would give a young man beginning to preach is work hard! If you work hard, everything else will find a way to work itself out.

4. *What wisdom would you give a young man who was thinking about getting into preaching? How can one know when to pull the plug with their decision?*

    For someone thinking about getting into preaching, I would say, don't do it just to have a job. Understand that this is more than a job. It is a lifestyle; it is a mission. Don't be a preacher if you just want a title, job, or position.

5. *How do you start your mornings to maximize your day?*

I start every morning with a period of planning and devotion. Since I have a type A personality, planning is easy for me to do. I believe if a preacher doesn't plan each day, he will allow his time to get away from him and it will show on Sunday.

6. *How do you start your week to maximize your time?*

I usually start my weeks by trying to knock out the things I have to do on Sunday. That is in case I have a funeral or series of hospital visits to do as the week goes on.

7. *What's the biggest challenge you've faced as a preacher? How did you handle it?*

The biggest challenge I have faced is worrying about things beyond my control. I have learned to just focus on what I can control and leave the rest in the Lord's hands.

8. *How does your wife help you in your ministry?*

My wife encourages me all the time and is excellent with people. She is super friendly and great at building relationships and enhancing my influence.

9. *How do you go about writing a sermon? Topic? Length?*

I write down every word for sermons and memorize the outline. I also believe in being organized in my thoughts and using slides. I keep a sermon log and always try to have balance in my preaching. I consult both with my co-worker in the gospel and the elders on sermon ideas. I have never found finding something to preach on hard because the Bible has 66 books and thousands of chapters. Finding something to preach about from a book like that should be easy to do! I usually preach between 34–38 minutes.

10. *What book have you gifted the most to people?*

I don't usually gift books. I have gifted to various elders: *They Smell Like Sheep.*

11. *What are some of your favorite books to read?*

    My favorite books to read are books about the work of preaching and books that give great summaries of Bible stories and periods in Bible history.

12. *When do you know when it's time to move to another work?*

    This question is hard to answer. When I was in Florida for 5 years, I left when I felt the church had become stagnant and the people needed to hear a new voice and someone with new ideas. It was really a case of the right church calling me at the right time!

13. *What advice would you give to other preachers when it comes to work/family balance?*

    When you go home, be home. Always make time for your family. Go on vacations with your family. Don't try to save the world and lose your family!

14. *Timothy had Paul as a mentor. Who was or is your Paul in the faith? In what ways were they able to help you?*

    Max Dawson was my Paul. He taught me about the value of hard work, trusting God, being there for people, and always giving God excellence.

15. *What piece of advice would you give when it comes to evangelism?*

    When it comes to evangelism, encourage the congregation to invite. If they can get the people through the doors, then you take it from there! Also, find ways to get into the community and meet people. The more people you meet and build relationships with, the more contacts you will build.

16. *How do you decide how many meetings to hold? When should you decline invitations? How do you go about declining invitations?*

    I usually hold 4–5 meetings a year. I try not to go past that because I want to use a couple of my weeks for vacation with my family. I have had to turn meetings down before. When I do, I just tell the truth. I tell the church that all my weeks are used up for the year and the elders only let me be gone for a certain amount.

Shawn Jeffries has been preaching at the Jackson Heights church of Christ in Columbia, TN, for over five years. Previously, he was in Leesburg, FL, for five years and at the Dowlen Road church in Beaumont, Texas, for two years.

Benjamin Lee

1. *How and when did you decide to get into preaching full time? What was your motivation or your WHY?*

I grew up in a really small church. When I say small, I mean 10 people small. My grandfather was the preacher. One of my grandfather's brothers was also a preacher. So from a young age, I was around preachers and I began to preach (if you want to call it that). My sister would actually help me put some thoughts together. I had no idea what I was doing. When I moved from Urbana, IL, to Rockford, IL, in 2001 for work, my preacher there got me interested in preaching. One day he asked if I could fill in for him and I said I would. Again, I had no idea what I was doing. I heard a sermon from someone else and preached it word for word (forgive me I have sinned)! It was called, "One More Night with the Frogs." A few months later that preacher came to hold a gospel meeting. I was so scared he would preach his sermon that I stole from him. Thankfully, he didn't. I really began to think about preaching in 2001, but it was in 2009 that I made the ultimate decision to get into it full time. Seeing the need for preachers was my motivation to get into it. I had prayed about this decision for years. I believe the other work I was doing in sales was preparing me to preach.

2. *As a preacher, have you always worked in a full-time setting capacity or have you been like Paul building tents from time to time?*

I worked with Pfizer Inc. as a healthcare representative from 2001–2009. During that time, I was preaching, teaching Bible classes, or setting up some kind of study in the community. In 2009, I began a preacher-training program at the Dowlen Road church of Christ in Beaumont, TX. From that time on, I have preached full time.

3. *What one piece of advice would you give a young man who has begun to preach?*

The one piece of advice I would give would be to strive for excellence. We serve an excellent God so He deserves our best.

Therefore, in all that we do (Bible class, sermon preparation, etc.) we should do our best. You always have room for improvement. Remember who it's all about: God!

4. *What wisdom would you give a young man who was thinking about getting into preaching? How can one know when to pull the plug with their decision?*

    First, I would say, "That's great that you're thinking about getting into preaching." Then I would ask, "What's your motivation or your *why* as to why you want to preach fulltime?" I would encourage the young man to truly count the cost. I would want him to understand the commitment that he's about to make. Before he pulls the plug and dives into preaching, I would want him to look at all aspects of his decision (how will he begin, what training he may need, his financial situation, his family situation, etc.) Then after doing that I would encourage him to pray and think about it some more. I took eight years to truly make the decision. Take your time and be confident in your decision. Don't do it because someone else wants you to.

5. *How do you start your mornings to maximize your day?*

    I began waking up at 4 a.m. in 2016. My friend wanted to workout at the gym at 5 each morning, so I had to wake up earlier. Eventually, we stopped working out in the morning, but I kept waking up early. I love it! It's like living two days in one. I don't always wake up at 4 a.m. but most of the time it's like clockwork. I will do the same thing on the weekends. If you sleep in on the weekends, it's tough to stick to that time during the week. Here's what I do:

    1. Some kind of caffeine first thing in the morning. Then I have 16 ounces of water with one lemon. Thirty minutes later, I will have a protein shake and my Athletic Greens Supplement.

    2. Next I will do some kind of journaling. I will write out my prayers. I will write out motivational thoughts to myself. I will blog or work on a book (It's 4:26 a.m. right now as I'm writing this).

3. Then I will workout (every preacher should be working out...No excuses...C'mon now...Get up). I will workout at home or at the gym (another way to meet people in the community) for 25–35 minutes. I will then get my day started at the building between 8–9 a.m.

6. *How do you start your week to maximize your time?*

I've started using the *Full Focus Planner* by Michael Hyatt. In it, there's a place to think about the biggest things that need to be accomplished for the week. I will start this process on Sunday. I work on Mondays. I want to get stuff done early because something always happens on Fridays. I don't like to work on Saturdays. I will run through my sermons again on Saturdays, but nothing major. They will have been written and completed by Thursday at the latest.

7. *What's the biggest challenge you've faced as a preacher? How did you handle it?*

As a preacher, there will be a lot of challenges. The challenge of losing members due to death, people disappointing you due to sinful actions, the devil putting roadblocks in your way with respect to evangelism, and so much more. The biggest? This may be the hardest to answer. I would say trusting in the Lord that He will provide for me. Having a heart condition and having two ICDs (Implantable Cardioverter Defibrillator) placed in my chest (first one in 2010 and second one in 2016). I've often worried about healthcare and how certain things would be paid. In 2016, I was thinking about stopping full-time preaching and doing some tent work due to certain health costs. At times I didn't handle it well. Thankfully, things worked out well.

8. *How does your wife help you in your ministry?*

My wife, Nikki, has been a great blessing to me. She assists me in various ways. She provides me with honest feedback on my teaching and preaching. She holds me accountable when it comes to saying no more. I have a hard time saying no, so she helps me to try to keep things balanced between work and family. She has been a great encouragement to me when I've been down.

9. *How do you go about writing a sermon? Topic? Length?*

When I was working at the Dowlen Road church, I worked with two other preachers. This required a lot of coordination on our part on Mondays and Tuesdays about preaching schedules and topics. As the only preacher at the West Main Church, I keep track of what I preach to ensure that there are various topics being discussed. Throughout the week, I will make sermon sketches. A sermon sketch is when I have an idea or some thoughts. I will write these down and store them for another time. I've begun writing sermons three weeks in advance so I can think about them more and to stay ahead of the game. I like to have my sermons finished by Thursday at the latest. I have a sermon template (If you want a copy, let me know). I try to stick to two pages. I will take these pages with me in the pulpit. This format helps me to keep things concise. If I ever want to preach that sermon again, I can simply pull out the outline and I will be ready to go. I try to preach between 25–30 minutes.

10. *What book have you gifted the most to people?*

I don't have one specific book. I have gifted books written by Lee Strobel, like *The Case for Christ*. There's a lot of great information in it (although he's wrong on how one receives salvation). I have also bought Dave Ramsey's book *Financial Peace* for members. I have also gifted Bibles to people. I'm really trying to work on this more.

11. *What are some of your favorite books to read?*

I love to read:

- The Bible.
- *Deep Work* by Cal Newport.
- *Real Artists Don't Starve* by Jeff Goin.
- *Financial Peace* by Dave Ramsey.
- *Discipline Equals Freedom: Field Manual* by Jocko Willink.
- *Tactics: A Game Plan for Discussing Your Christian Convictions* by Gregory Koukl.
- *I Don't Have Enough Faith to be an Atheist* by Frank Turek.
- All material by Wilson Adams.

- *Take the Risk* by Ben Carson.
- *Speak Like Churchill Stand Like Lincoln* by James Humes.

12. *When do you know when it's time to move to another work?*

I spent eight years at my first work. It was really hard leaving. Knowing when it's time to leave will vary depending on the person and situation. I took eight years to begin preaching. I took a long time really thinking about the decision that I made to leave. One of the big reasons for me was the opportunity to assist another congregation I feel I can help grow. Another big reason for me was the opportunity to preach in a different format. Many preachers and congregations are going to a two-preacher format, which is great. I began working in a three-preacher format and periodically a two-preacher format. There are great benefits of these arrangements. I wanted to experience a different format. With any decision, there are a number of factors that must be considered (family dynamics, effectiveness, financial factors, etc.).

13. *What advice would you give to other preachers when it comes to work/family balance?*

You need to work hard and keep track of your hours. You need to take all of your vacation every year. You need to spend plenty of time with family. You need to get away with family. Don't feel bad. The work will be fine. Don't preach about the importance of family and then never spend time with yours.

14. *Timothy had Paul as a mentor. Who was or is your Paul in the faith?* In what ways were they able to help you?

I mentioned this in the introduction but I will mention it again. Max Dawson and David Banning have been the two biggest influences for me as mentors. Coming to the Dowlen Road church and going through the preaching-training program was a great decision.

15. *What piece of advice would you give when it comes to evangelism?*

Reaching the lost is not rocket science. You can be successful. Remain upbeat and help the congregation develop a culture of evangelism. Preach on it regularly, have Bible classes dealing with evangelism, and take the lead. Keep invite cards on you and determine to get at least five cards out each week. Make yourself available for evening Bible studies. Remember that evangelism is a team effort. You need the members and they need you.

16. *How do you decide how many meetings to hold? When should you decline invitations? How do you go about declining invitations?*

When I first started preaching, I would accept any meeting that I was invited to. I'm beginning to change my approach. Having a young son, I want to be around for him more. My wife also has a busy schedule, which plays a factor if I can yes or no. I can do four meetings a year. I've taken advice given to me from Jeff Wilson about scheduling. I'm trying to schedule all of my meetings either in the spring or the fall, to cut down on being away from home all throughout the year. Declining meetings will vary depending on your situation. I had a blood clot in my heart in June 2014. I cancelled the rest of my meetings that year. The brethren understood. You should decline meetings if they get in the way of your work at your congregation. A lot of work has to go into meetings, which takes away time from your local work. When your wife says, "You're gone too much" is when you should begin to decline meetings. There's a danger for preachers to let the number of meetings to go their heads. Don't get too high on yourself if you have meetings. Don't get too low on yourself if you don't have meetings. They come and go.

Benjamin Lee has been preaching the gospel since 2009. After working for several years for Pfizer Pharmaceuticals, Benjamin devoted his life to preaching the gospel. He and his wife, Nikki, moved to Beaumont, TX, in July 2009, where he began working in the evangelist-in-training program under the instruction of the elders and evangelists at Dowlen Road. He began the work of a full-time evangelist with Dowlen Road in July 2011–February 2018.

Benjamin began working with the West Main church of Christ in Lewisville, TX, on March 1, 2018. He and his wife have been married for 14 years. They have a seven-year old son named Joshua. Benjamin is passionate about faith, family, and fitness. He has had the opportunity to preach and teach in Africa, Mexico, and throughout the United States. His blog and other books can be found at www.benjaminleeonline.com.

Justin McCorkle

1. *How and when did you decide to get into preaching full time? What was your motivation or your WHY?*

Working at my first part-time work while in college was a challenge. I was driving two and a half hours each way twice per week to take care of my teaching and preaching obligations. My wife and I were still in college, although I was only a few months from graduation, when a local congregation invited me full support to work with them. It was a perfect situation since my wife had over a year left in school, so I accepted the invitation. I stayed with the congregation for six years. I had never made a conscious decision to continue preaching full time for my life's work, I just looked up one day and realized that's what I was doing.

2. *As a preacher, have you always worked in a full-time setting capacity or have you been like Paul building tents from time to time?*

While the income provided from the congregation at my first full-time work was sufficient for a college student, having a family and desiring things like a house caused me to seek additional income. At various times, I did substitute teaching, kept up yards for a neighborhood association, worked at a boat dealership, etc.

3. *What one piece of advice would you give a young man who has begun to preach?*

Become a professional at what you are doing. That is to say, don't improvise it. Learn what is working for other churches and preachers. Imitate those that you admire. Push yourself to be the best you can be at what you are doing, including presenting lessons and teaching the gospel. If you do not push yourself, it is not likely anyone else will push you, either.

4. *What wisdom would you give a young man who was thinking about getting into preaching? How can one know when to pull the plug with their decision?*

Being a true evangelist is much more than presenting lessons from the pulpit. In my experience, we have nine baptisms outside of service times for every one during them. If you want to spread the gospel, you have to do it at the kitchen table. Your weekly schedule should reflect that reality. If you are not self-motivated, zealous for evangelism, humble enough to learn from those already doing the work how you would like to do it, and if your spouse is not fully on board with your decision to preach, pull the plug.

5. *How do you start your mornings to maximize your day?*

My schedule is heavily weighted toward the evenings. Every morning I wake up with my children and spend some time with them, then I exercise by running or hitting the gym. After cleaning up, I will be at the office usually around 10 a.m.

6. *How do you start your week to maximize your time?*

I use Mondays to take care of tasks that I know will likely otherwise not be done if pushed to later in the week, such as writing this up. I will try to work on extra projects (monthly goals) that do not fall into a normal weekly schedule. I know my weekly work will get done (such as lesson preparation), so I save it for later in the week. I start the week with important tasks that can easily be pushed off forever if not paid attention to.

7. *What's the biggest challenge you've faced as a preacher? How did you handle it?*

My biggest challenge has been, and continues to be, allowing the numerous activities of the church and among members to come between time with family. By family, I do not even simply refer to my immediate family, but also to my parents, grandparents, and sibling. There are always things going on such as get togethers, home studies, funerals, weddings, etc. And as a preacher you will likely not live close to your extended family. Months or more pass without setting aside time to visit loved ones. I know I will regret that. The best advice I can currently give is to try and schedule time for those things in advance and treat them as you do other unmovable engagements.

8. *How does your wife help you in your ministry?*

The older I become, the less I ask of my wife regarding my work. It is harder for her to bear some of the difficulties I face as a preacher than it is for me. She helps me through being hospitable and having her personal relationships with women of the church, but I seek more to have her not feel the pressures of being the preacher's wife. She is a Christian woman and that should be enough for the church.

9. *How do you go about writing a sermon? Topic? Length?*

Inspiration for lessons comes primarily through reading. Any time I come across a thought or passage I think worthy of a sermon, I immediately put the thought down. Other times a topic just needs to be discussed, so I will reverse my approach by doing specific reading and looking for the thought that excites me and then expounding on it. I like my sermons not to exceed 35 minutes in length.

10. *What book have you gifted the most to people?*

I have often gifted David Bercot's *Will the Real Heretics Please Stand Up*. It's easy to read and introduces people to the early Christian writings, which I find very beneficial.

11. *What are some of your favorite books to read?*

The Training of the Twelve by A.B. Bruce, *The Ante-Nicene Writings*, and David deSilva's works are among my favorite books. Leadership and time management books are also always valuable and in a rotation on my list.

12. *When do you know when it's time to move to another work?*

Having just recently left a wonderful work and congregation, I still can't say I'm fully able to answer that question. Sometimes you have to go, sometimes you want to go, and sometimes you feel you need to go. My recent move was the latter. I saw a need in this congregation that I think I can help fill, potential for the work in the area, and family circumstances (closer relatives) that gave additional appeal. Don't be hasty to leave.

13. *What advice would you give to other preachers when it comes to work/family balance?*

Learn the power of no. It is difficult to not go to the things brethren ask you to go to. Even other preachers will often try to guilt you into attending all of the area meetings, etc. Your time is valuable to your family as well. Do what you can comfortably do without making your family feel neglected. Say no to the rest.

14. *Timothy had Paul as a mentor. Who was or is your Paul in the faith? In what ways were they able to help you?*

I've had mentors in different seasons and for different reasons. Listing here names of preachers that have helped me in various ways quickly became long, and worry increased that I would forget some important brother. Besides preachers, I have been blessed to have several elders and brethren that have taken me under their wings.

15. *What piece of advice would you give when it comes to evangelism?*

Get rid of the negative mantra in your mind that brethren always say. "People don't want the gospel," "people are different around here," etc. People don't want the traditions and baggage we can tend to tie onto the gospel, but they want the gospel... they just don't know it yet. Look at what is working in other congregations. We use a version of *The Big Picture* with great success and other churches are growing with other tools for teaching. There's no need to come up with a way on your own. Be humble enough to adopt what is working at other places.

16. *How do you decide how many meetings to hold? When should you decline invitations? How do you go about declining invitations?*

Fewer meetings is better for my schedule. It seems prudent to decline meetings where the goal is unclear. What is the church seeking to accomplish with my coming? What is the topic they desire, if there is one? Because I hold few meetings, declining meetings politely is usually as simple as explaining that my schedule is already full.

Justin McCorkle is 33 years old and has been preaching full time for 12 years at the time of publication. He is currently working with the Southside Church in Jacksonville, TX. He is married to Kelly and is a father of three. Justin is also an avid runner and adventure sports enthusiast.

Shane Millard

1. *How and when did you decide to get into preaching full time? What was your motivation or your WHY?*

Mine was kind of different than some people. I did my first invitation and was asked about doing a lesson at a really small country church. I went and did that and started doing it on a rotating basis, about once a month usually. That led into other opportunities and so on. I never had that *I have to preach* moment. But I did know I wanted to have a life that had meaning and that helped other people. That could be achieved by being a doctor or something else like that. But I was thinking that I wanted to do something that would benefit people forever—that's what made me want to preach. As I've grown, I've realized that there are plenty of ways you can impact people forever. But that was my initial motivation and it still influences me today.

2. *As a preacher, have you always worked in a full-time setting capacity or have you been like Paul building tents from time to time?*

I have worked part time during the time I was doing my preacher training, and I did some part-time work during my first full-time work (I was also going to school during both of those times).

3. *What one piece of advice would you give a young man who has begun to preach?*

Humility. I know that attribute is essential to enter the kingdom and I believe it is essential to be a preacher. Humility will help you to not come in and tell a church all the things they are doing wrong and that you in your wisdom know better than them. Humility will keep you constantly learning and wanting advice to help you be better. Humility will help you realize you can be wrong on an issue and that you need to listen to the truth on it. Humility will keep you from preaching for your pride and money, and will help you focus on God and His approval. It just seems like a systemic approach that will always yield fruit. But it seems to be one thing that can be missing with preachers and when it is, it destroys so many things.

4. *What wisdom would you give a young man who was thinking about getting into preaching? How can one know when to pull the plug with their decision?*

I grew up hearing the whole "If you can do anything other than preach, then don't preach." I just don't know that I completely agree with that. There are plenty of places in churches where you can preach and do a work that you enjoy. But I will say this, preaching is hard at times. It is not an easy way to a paycheck. You have to have a strong desire to do it, but you don't have to do it forever. If you're wanting to do it but you're not sure if it's a permanent thing, then perhaps you should commit to a certain amount of time, or perhaps two works (since usually the first work is hard because you don't know much and the options you get aren't usually the best).

As for when to pull the plug, if it's destroying your family, you, or the church, please stop. But, sometimes people are doing good work and they just want to stop. I don't know that there is one single sign that tells you that you need to quit. But if you don't enjoy the work (even though its hard sometimes), then do something else. If you can be happy doing something else, then feel free to do that. My one tip of advice though is this—never decide to quit preaching when the situations are bad and never decide to keep preaching when things are good. You need to critically evaluate when things are somewhere in the middle.

5. *How do you start your mornings to maximize your day?*

I start with Bible reading and prayer almost every morning. I didn't do this for years while I was preaching. It's a habit that I started last year, and it has been very rewarding and helpful.

6. *How do you start your week to maximize your time?*

I try to work Monday every week. If you wait till Tuesday, you get behind and it can be a struggle to get the rest of the work done.

7. *What's the biggest challenge you've faced as a preacher? How did you handle it?*

It was getting into a work that I should not have gone to. I didn't have the experience that I needed to handle the situation well and the church had a lot of problems that were not my own creation. That compounded with my lack of humility in some ways and led to a very difficult situation.

How I handled it was me trying to help the situation, which I felt like I did. But for some of those good things I did, there were other bad decisions I made. It ultimately led to where I ended up leaving the work. So, perhaps for someone, maybe the answer is to realize a situation is over your head and move on.

8. *How does your wife help you in your ministry?*

This could go on for quite a while. My wife is my constant encouragement and helper, as well as a helpful critic. She helps with the classes for the children and builds relationships with the other ladies with the church. She helps me to know how to handle difficult situations better. She helps me to be holy by having someone to meet with other women with. It really just goes on and on. You can preach without a wife and in some ways can be more effective. But having a wife can make a lot of things much easier. It's all a trade-off.

9. *How do you go about writing a sermon? Topic? Length?*

Usually I try to keep things pretty simple, 3–5 points and from one main text. Many of my lessons come from something I've been reading or studying, or maybe an idea or a lesson of a friend. Usually I have a plan for what lessons I'm going to be doing, so I have some general ideas of things I want to talk about. I may compile some resources or texts knowing that I want to talk about it in the future. I believe one of the things that helps is having some preparation before and a plan.

As for topic, it's going to vary; I think having a plan will help you to be balanced and have a good approach. But often a topic comes from something I'm interested in or something the church needs.

Length is usually about 35 minutes or less. I think less than 30 would be much better for younger guys especially. They're easier to listen to and force you to be concise.

10. *What book have you gifted the most to people?*

I don't gift a lot of books to people and the ones I have were all about the same amount (about three people). But a book I keep gifting people is *How to Stop Worrying and Start Living* by Dale Carnegie; it's just so critical for how to manage stress and be able to enjoy work and life, which becomes a huge problem as a preacher.

11. *What are some of your favorite books to read?*

Just about anything by Dale Carnegie. I have really enjoyed works by Tim Keller, John Maxwell, Steven Covey, Carey Nieuwhof, Thom Rainer, etc. I think there is a lot of wisdom in people that are in the business world or have experiences which other churches and belief systems. Reading different resources helps you to approach things differently. But be warned—they are wrong on a lot of things and you should probably know their background biblically before reading them.

12. *When do you know when it's time to move to another work?*

When the next church calls! In all seriousness, this is a very difficult question. I was told once that whenever you leave you will never feel like the work is done. I think there is a lot of truth in that. If you're having an impasse on very important topics then that might be a sign. If you're having conflict and it's damaging the church then that might be a sign. If you're in a situation that is really causing a problem for your family then that's a very strong sign. Ultimately you have to evaluate the various signs and decide what is best for your family. Keep in mind the grass is not always greener on the other side and sometimes it's much better to simply water the grass you're on instead of moving. You always take your attitude with you and if your attitude is poor, then changing works won't change that.

13. *What advice would you give to other preachers when it comes to work/family balance?*

Most of the advice I give to others is advice I have received from other people. I have heard from others that the Lord does not expect us to save the world and lose our family. I think there is a lot of value in that. Recently I read where Paul Earnhardt said, "Lots of men can substitute for you as a preacher, but no one can substitute for you as a husband or a father" (Paul Earnhart via Jason Hardin). With those things in mind, I think you have to choose your priorities, which is the most important. Then schedule your priorities (when will you be with family, work, etc.) and realize that a lot of things will go undone (sometimes following up with leads, etc.) and you'll have to be okay with some of that. You can only do so much and you have to be able to sustain yourself for the long haul and not burn out.

14. *Timothy had Paul as a mentor. Who was or is your Paul in the faith? In what ways were they able to help you?*

Jim McDonald is probably my biggest mentor. He was the one who taught me so much over the years and while I was in the training program in Lufkin. But I have had so many mentors because I realize the value of them and I seek them out. It is because of these men that I am who I am. I'm deeply grateful for the advice and I would say young men absolutely have to have them. Jim has helped me with understanding Bible texts, how to handle issues, answering my questions, and helping me find churches to work with. Mentors are just so valuable.

15. *What piece of advice would you give when it comes to evangelism?*

Work on getting more people involved in the process. Train people to teach and invite; make it a culture in the church. If you get where you feel like you're the only one doing evangelism and that the growth of the church relies on you, that's a terrible and unbiblical position to be in.

16. *How do you decide how many meetings to hold? When should you decline invitations? How do you go about declining invitations?*

Usually that is decided when I go to a church; that's a normal discussion topic when you go to work with a new church. You should decline invitations obviously if you don't have the time, but you could always ask the brethren for a special situation. I've never had to decline a meeting invitation since I don't usually do that many. But if I thought it would cause problems with the church there or the church where I am, I would seriously consider not doing the meeting.

I would try to handle it respectfully and if there is a reason that you feel like you can/needs to be discussed, then do that. I think you'll have to talk to other people for better answers on this one.

Shane Millard was born and raised in Nacogdoches, TX. He met Alina Whitehorn at Stephen F. Austin State University, and they were married in 2011. They have two children, Jude and Catherine. They are expecting a third child.

Shane started preaching at small congregations near his home, and then spent over two years in a preacher-training program at the Loop 287 church of Christ in Lufkin, TX. He has worked as a located, full-time preacher since 2013 with the Southside church in Greenville, TX, and the Milam Street church in Jasper, TX. Shane recently began working with the North Hixson church of Christ in Hixson, TN, in May 2018. In addition to this, Shane had the opportunity to work in the Philippines on short trips two different times.

Shane is passionate about his family, sports, and especially his faith. He is passionate about God and proclaiming His Word faithfully in an easy to understand and applicable way.

Brent Moody

1. *How and when did you decide to get into preaching full time? What was your motivation or your WHY?*

I preached for the first time when I was 18. My grandpa signed me up to preach on my way through Chattanooga to Florida College. I hadn't given it much thought prior to this, but I loved the whole process. My father preached full time my whole life, so I understood many aspects of the work. I'm not sure the exact moment I decided to preach, but it wasn't long after my first sermon.

2. *As a preacher, have you always worked in a full-time setting capacity or have you been like Paul building tents from time to time?*

I have always preached full time.

3. *What one piece of advice would you give a young man who has begun to preach?*

Always focus on progress. A growing preacher will best equip the congregation. Study habits, sermons, teaching, and interpersonal skills can always improve. Listen to, evaluate, and welcome criticism. Don't be thin skinned. Find a preacher who does his job well and learn everything you can from him.

4. *What wisdom would you give a young man who was thinking about getting into preaching? How can one know when to pull the plug with their decision?*

You need to ask "is this the best way I can serve in the kingdom?" Preaching is not the only way to have a major influence. You have to love the work. Good study is hard work and you have to really enjoy it. If you just love talking and not studying, don't preach.

5. *How do you start your mornings to maximize your day?*

My goal is to wake up each morning at 6 a.m. I spend 45–60 minutes doing a mixture of prayer, mediation, visualizing my day, reading, journaling, and exercise.

6. *How do you start your week to maximize your time?*

I work on Monday. Whenever I take Monday off I regret it, unless it is for family reasons. It is a terrible way to start the week. I do busy work, read, or general planning, but I try to do something on Monday.

7. *What's the biggest challenge you've faced as a preacher? How did you handle it?*

Deciding whether or not to work at home. Our schedule is such a great benefit, but it can be a challenge to do good work at home. I finally decided I do my best work at the office. I still work at home at times, but not often. It is too hard to concentrate with children needing attention. House chores become easy distractions. Every interruption makes you significantly less productive.

8. *How does your wife help you in your ministry?*

Before children, she provided great feedback and constructive criticism. Let your wife critique you. She will tell you the truth because she loves you and wants you do to the best job you can. Katie has always been aware of the little things that can help me improve.

9. *How do you go about writing a sermon? Topic? Length?*

I write down ideas whenever I have them. I also do a three-month sermon planner with a mixture of topical and textual sermons. My outlines are typically 1–2 pages long. My goal is to only preach 30 minutes.

10. *What book have you gifted the most to people?*

Do Hard Things

11. *What are some of your favorite books to read?*

- *Essentialism: The Disciplined Pursuit of Less.*
- *The Miracle Morning.*
- *Mere Christianity.*

- *Dumbing Us Down: The Hidden Curriculum of Compulsory Schooling.*
- *Speak like Churchill, Stand Like Lincoln*—every preacher should read this.

12. *When do you know when it's time to move to another work?*

There is no reason to randomly leave a good work. If you do your work well, you can do good work in one place for 20+ years. If an opportunity arises that you feel drawn to, it may be worth taking. If where you are is not supporting you well enough, it may also be time to move. Preachers need to take care of their family just like anyone else.

13. *What advice would you give to other preachers when it comes to work/family balance?*

Leave your work at the office as much as possible. Our schedule is flexible, but do not get drawn into every family activity during the week. This will ensure that work comes home. Your wife may think she wants you involved during the week, but it is not good for anyone when it feels like you are working every day, but not getting much done. Get your work done efficiently, and have committed time with the family.

14. *Timothy had Paul as a mentor. Who was or is your Paul in the faith? In what ways were they able to help you?*

I worked with Dee Bowman in the preaching program at Southside church of Christ. We started out with the basics of writing good sermons and good work ethic. By the end of the two years, more time was spent on interpersonal skills. A lot of people struggle in their work because they do not learn how to interact properly with people.

15. *What piece of advice would you give when it comes to evangelism?*

Every person and congregation is different. Trying to copy what someone else does rarely works. Be yourself and live your message. Encourage the congregation to be involved in the process; they often have much better contacts than preachers who often aren't even from the cities they live in.

16. *How do you decide how many meetings to hold? When should you decline invitations? How do you go about declining invitations?*

I only hold three meetings per year. It was part of what was agreed upon when I moved to Kleinwood. I decline meeting invitations if it doesn't work out for my schedule.

Brent worked in a two-year training program with Dee Bowman at the Southside church of Christ in Pasadena, TX, from 2004–2006. He preached at the Helena congregation near Birmingham, AL, and at the Bartlett congregation near Memphis, TN, prior to moving to the Kleinwood church of Christ in 2014.

Brent received an AA degree from Florida College (2002), a B.S. in Financial Planning from Western Kentucky University (2004), and a M.A. in New Testament from Harding School of Theology (2014).

David Osteen

1. *How and when did you decide to get into preaching full time? What was your motivation or your WHY?*

Just about any young man who has an ability and a willingness to stand in front of a group of Christians and teach will begin to get pressure to become a preacher. The pressure really just comes in the form of encouragement. From the encouragement begins to develop expectations, that is, the expectations of the encouragers and that comes from a few sources:

1. Need—Brethren recognize we need good workers, and yet someone really smart once said, "The harvest is plentiful, but the workers are few." All honest brethren can look at the world around us and see the truth of that statement.

2. Pride—Even though the old proverb "a prophet is not without honor except in his hometown," as that prophet goes out he can bring honor to his hometown. If he does good work, which they obviously believe he can (after all, they taught him in their Bible class), there definitely will be some pride among those brethren if the young man takes up the calling to be a preacher. Their calling that is.

3. Responsibility—Brethren have the expectation that young men respond to their ability. Use their talents. A man who has all ability in the world to preach will get some sideways stares and discouraging discussions if he has the ability to preach, but chooses not to. Of course, to the young man, he then may pursue the profession out of guilt. But should that be his motivation? Not for a preacher. If one is going to be a preacher, it should be out of passion: a passion for God, a passion for God's people, a passion for people, period! A passion for the gospel. A passion for truth. A young man, or any man for that matter, who is deciding to be a preacher, if it's not because of passion then it will difficult for him to truly do the work of an evangelist. Not the work of printing a bulletin each week, preaching two sermons, and holding down

two classes, but doing the work of an evangelist. (Note: Acts; I & II Timothy; Titus.)

I didn't really know at the time why I was deciding to be a preacher. I just did. For me, it was part of my Christian growth and maturity. I had the passion, but I didn't know it at the time, nor did I know that should be my reason and my motivation. I'm thankful that by the grace and patience of God, He allowed me to understand why I should've decided to preach full-time, and why I did.

2. *As a preacher, have you always worked in a full-time setting capacity or have you been like Paul building tents from time to time?*

I've never thought about building tents, but I've thought about building parachutes a few times. Or perhaps safety nets would be a more apt analogy. The reason being, because the person who has a safety net still has faith, it's just a responsible faith. The Lord wants His servants to be responsible. That means, doing what you need to do for the care and well being of those entrusted to you—your family. Preaching has always been my number one work, my full-time work. No other tent making or safety net sewing has ever taken precedence over my work for the Lord. I'm most thankful though, in the graciousness of God's servants in providing for my work, that those needs for additional secular work have been few and far between. God's people are gracious, kind, supporting, loving, and generous in each of those respects. I firmly believe if you are committed to the work as you should be, the Lord does provide. Oftentimes in meaningful, powerful, surprising ways. Glory be to God!

3. *What one piece of advice would you give a young man who has begun to preach?*

Run. Run and don't look back. Only kidding of course. This is it. If the greatest command is to "Love the Lord your God with all of your heart, all of your soul, all of your mind, and all of your strength," and all the law can be summed up in this one word—love. Love is the greatest of all, then the rest of my life in ministry needs to be devoted to learning more about what that one word means and how to live it and teach it to others. Everything else I learn and do needs to come from there. Love. If you spend the rest of your life in ministry learning what love is and how to properly apply and how to effectively teach it to others then you will fulfill your ministry from God.

4. *What wisdom would you give a young man who was thinking about getting into preaching? How can one know when to pull the plug with their decision?*

To the guy who is always thinking about being a preacher but can't seem to pull the trigger just remember, would you be ok with your tombstone reading, "Almost dedicated his life to being a gospel preacher"? If not, then pull the trigger.

Don't let your fears be greater than your faith. If you really can't do the work, then don't do it. If you really don't want to do the work then, don't do it. If you can't handle brethren joking about your work not really being work, then don't do it. If you are waiting for a sign, you are not a worker, you are an astrologer. If you love the Lord, if you love His people, if you love the work, then the only regret you will have is not having started sooner.

5. *How do you start your mornings to maximize your day?*

I wake up and get out of bed.

6. *How do you start your week to maximize your time?*

Lots of coffee. (Not true. My body is actually intolerant of coffee.) I start it at 5 a.m. Sunday morning filled with a full day of worshipping God with brethren of like faith. What better way to start the week? Perhaps that's why the Lord prescribed it.

7. *What's the biggest challenge you've faced as a preacher? How did you handle it?*

I would love to say I handled it with dignity and grace. That might depend on whose perspective. You'll always face challenges: money, time, or challenges from brethren such as dishonesty, discouragement, disdain, etc. But the biggest challenge I will always face is living what I know. Being who I know I should be as a husband, father, son, brother, Christian, evangelist, neighbor, etc. Learning is easy. Living up to the expectations of what you learn, that's a challenge.

8. *How does your wife help you in your ministry?*

    She stays married to me. She loves me. She grows in her love for me (even when I don't deserve it). She works and she grows spiritually. She manages the household effectively and only calls upon me for what she needs help with. She loves our children and our family. She loves God's people. She takes my kids to the nursery when they're misbehaving during my sermon so that I don't have to do it. Every Sunday evening after a long hard day of work, she gives me a shoulder massage (well, not yet, but I hope maybe that'll be a part of her growth and love). Every day I live, I know I'm blessed to have her. I'm not worthy to have her. She's a constant companion, a faithful helpmeet, a steadfast servant, a hard worker, and a beautiful soul. She gives me peace in all of my work in the ministry.

9. *How do you go about writing a sermon? Topic? Length?*

    Carefully in every aspect.

10. *What book have you gifted the most to people?*

    Aside from the Bible, *Muscle and a Shovel*, Bullinger's *Figures of Speech*, and Vine's *Expository Dictionary*.

11. *What are some of your favorite books to read?*

    Non-fiction best sellers. I like interesting things written in interesting ways. Sometimes it being written in an interesting way is what makes an otherwise uninteresting topic interesting. "Do you see someone skilled in their work. They will serve before kings..." (Proverbs 22:29). Not to say I am a king. Just that, good works tend to rise to top. So, I typically like the cream of the crop, best sellers.

12. *When do you know when it's time to move to another work?*

When they tell me it's time. I'm not always good with subtlety. So when they tell me, then I know for sure it's time.

13. *What advice would you give to other preachers when it comes to work/family balance?*

Your work is your life. It will demand you at all different hours and in all different ways. It becomes a part of you, who you are. But your family is also your life. All of these statements also apply to your family. Therefore, do the best you can. Be conscious. Be aware. Be present. Sometimes you will feel like you are failing at one or the other or both. Probably rarely you will feel like you are hitting the balance perfectly all the time (or perhaps that's just my own unique self-critique). Do the best you can. Don't be too hard on yourself. Just make sure you are always communicating with both your church and your family about how you are trying the best you can to maintain the balance, and don't be afraid to let them know you may need their help when you truly do.

14. *Timothy had Paul as a mentor. Who was or is your Paul in the faith? In what ways were they able to help you?*

There is not just one. There are many, and if I start trying to list them all I will leave some off. Phil Arnold is one because he helped me choose to preach by telling me I didn't have to preach. Steve Fontenot is one because he was the preacher where my family attended for all of my formative years as a teenager. Don Hooton has always been a beloved friend, wise counselor, and trusted confidant. Warren Berkley and Mark Roberts have encouraged me through their work with Young Preachers Workshop. Again, there's well over a dozen other men who have helped me and/or mentored me in some form or fashion.

For me, in my work, my greatest help, however, has not been my Paul, but my Barnabas. (Or perhaps I should say Baranabases, but I'm not exactly sure how to make that plural.) Though not a preacher, Jerry Courtney has been one of my best friends since the 4th grade. He came to my house on December 4, 1994, with two beloved Christian friends and shared with me the gospel of Jesus Christ. We also both preached our first sermons on the same night of a meeting and did a lot of fill-in work together. Kris Emerson has been my best friend for 20 years. We started preaching together in Cleveland, TX, and have always remained close no matter how far apart. Aside from my own family, there is no one who has helped me more in my work for the Lord than Kris and Sommer and their family. They have always been the encouragers that I needed. They always will be. It's who they are. Anybody who knows them, knows that about them. I'm no Paul by any stretch, but nonetheless, I'm thankful for all the Barnabases the Lord has richly blessed me with through the years.

15. *What piece of advice would you give when it comes to evangelism?*

    Passion (see answer 1).

16. *How do you decide how many meetings to hold? When should you decline invitations? How do you go about declining invitations?*

    Ha! 1) As many as you are asked too without neglecting your family or your local work (magic number seems to be 4 to 6); 2) You should decline invitations when you cannot fulfill the work requested or it compromises your responsibilities at home; and 3) With grace and class.

David Osteen was raised in Humble, TX, ironically, a small town full of great pride outside of Houston, TX. He is a distant cousin of Joel Osteen (that may or may not be true), but was raised knowing (unlike Joel) that hermeneutics is not a Harry Potter character.

David is a college graduate in Interdisciplinary Studies from the University of Houston Downtown. He is also an Eagle Scout. However, David's greatest secular accomplishment is handily beating Benjamin Lee in a head-to-head battle for Best Speaker in Toastmasters competition (and has the ribbon and photo to prove it).

David is the blessed husband of the sweet, graceful, and elegant Adriana Osteen, who is the mother of their three amazing children: Joshua, Melanie Grace, and Kadry (pronounced Kay-dree). They are overjoyed to work with the O'Connor Road church of Christ in San Antonio, TX.

David's writings have been published in *Expository Files, Biblical Insights*, and *Pressing On* magazine as well as in various local church bulletins. He was also a contributor to *C.H.R.I.S.T.I.A.N.I.T.Y. in Twelve Words* and considers it a great honor to contribute to this work, to which he hopes to pass on to others the same encouragement he has been blessed with in his life and work.

Gabriel F. Puente

1. *How and when did you decide to get into preaching full time? What was your motivation or your WHY?*

   At 13, I knew I wanted to be a preacher because of the example of my father and other brothers. I began to preach at 16 at the local congregation, in Ojinaga, Chihuahua. At 22, God granted me a full-time preacher position in Santa Barbara, Chihuahua, where my father had started a new congregation and there was no male brother to stay in that city. My motivation comes from the great need for more workers dedicated to preaching and to the places where the gospel has not arrived.

2. *As a preacher, have you always worked in a full-time setting capacity or have you been like Paul building tents from time to time?*

   Occasionally, when we have needed more resources, we have sold used clothing (in garage sales), and my wife sells jewelry. But it has been temporary.

3. *What one piece of advice would you give a young man who has begun to preach?*

   Continue to improve every day, always listen, and learn from spiritual brothers and from those with more experience. That is not conformist. Also, do not allow criticism or too many compliments to affect your ministry. Criticism can cause discouragement, and too much praise can make you proud.

4. *What wisdom would you give a young man who was thinking about getting into preaching? How can one know when to pull the plug with their decision?*

   Meditate well and consider your motivations well. The life of a preacher, together with his family is not easy, but well rewarded. In preaching, one suffers but also enjoys oneself. Preaching the gospel faithfully will always be a wise decision. In my work as a preacher, I always remember <u>Psalm 126:5–6</u>, "Those who put in seed with weeping will get in the grain with cries of joy. Though a man may go out weeping, taking his vessel of seed with him; he

will come again in joy, with the corded stems of grain in his arms."
If he is married, he must have the support of his wife and family
because without it there will be conflict.

5. *How do you start your mornings to maximize your day?*

   I start with a prayer. Then I take my children to school, return for
   lunch, and then I go into my office to review the activities for the
   day.

6. *How do you start your week to maximize your time?*

   I write down the activities for each day and distribute my hours of
   the day as follows: I prepare material to publish on my website
   and in the bimonthly newsletter that I edit; I prepare material to
   distribute in the neighborhood, since I go out three times a week;
   and I prepare for home studies. Right now, I have only one study
   with a non-believer. I also prepare sermons for the church.

7. *What's the biggest challenge you've faced as a preacher? How did
   you handle it?*

   Dealt with carnal brothers who do not want to submit to the will of
   God, especially when the family favors him. I have handled this
   challenge by asking God for wisdom and patience, then spoke to
   the brother to try to correct him with patience, as Paul says to
   Timothy (2 Timothy 2:25).

8. *How does your wife help you in your ministry?*

   My wife helps me a lot in my work, giving me suggestions of topics
   to preach and teach. Eight years ago, she encouraged me to start a
   bulletin that I send to brothers in several countries via email. This
   also helps me publish my website regularly. She accompanies me
   to biblical studies in homes and visits.

9. *How do you go about writing a sermon? Topic? Length?*

   I usually prepare thematic sermons according to the needs of the
   congregation. I do a thematic sketch of an average of 1150 words,
   to present in 45 minutes.

10. *What book have you gifted the most to people?*

The New Testament has been the book that I have most given to people when I go out to knock on doors. I have realized that not everyone has the Bible, nor the New Testament. I have given the members a little book that I did when I began to preach, which is entitled *Comparative Biblical Studies*.

11. *What are some of your favorite books to read?*

The homiletic books are my favorite, books of articles written by experienced brothers that teach on the preaching and the work of the preacher. I also like John C. Maxwell's books like *Be all you Can Be* and *Failing Forward*.

12. *When do you know when it's time to move to another work?*

In a positive way, when in the congregation there are many mature brothers who work well in the local church, you may see that there is more need somewhere else. In a negative way, when a church is apathetic toward preaching and does not want to make changes.

13. *What advice would you give to other preachers when it comes to work/family balance?*

Try to plan your time so that you do not neglect your ministry nor your family. Sometimes we make the mistake of devoting a lot of time to a particular function that we neglect another. The preacher cares for all the people; we try to save souls, with greater reason must worry about the well-being, physical, emotional, and above all spiritual needs of our family.

14. *Timothy had Paul as a mentor. Who was or is your Paul in the faith? In what ways were they able to help you?*

Several brothers have given me good advice. My father, Ramón Puente, has been my mentor, from whom I learned to write my first sermons and use reference books. Also my father, in the difficult moments, has given me words of strength to continue in preaching. Through my father, I knew the way of God.

15. *What piece of advice would you give when it comes to evangelism?*

The work of evangelism is very important because it allows us to approach people, and to gain their trust, we must be attentive to people and know how to listen to them. If you learn to listen to people, they will be more willing to listen to what we have to say to them. It is also very important that the preacher has a humble attitude that does not leave the impression of superiority.

16. *How do you decide how many meetings to hold? When should you decline invitations? How do you go about declining invitations?*

I accept four to five meetings per year, but without neglecting the preaching work of the local church. I would not accept a meeting when I know that some false doctrine is taught there, or that there is a moral problem that is tolerated and does not want to be corrected. When I reject a series, I give the corresponding explanations according to the case.

Gabriel Puente was born in Ojinaga, Mexico, and is 38 years old. He was baptized into Christ at age 10. In 2002, he decided to become an evangelist. He has preached the gospel in two places where there is no church, in Santa Barbara, Chihuahua, for four years and in Jiménez, Chihuahua, for eight years, trying to establish new congregations. Gabriel has preached in Mexico and the United States in Spanish-speaking congregations.

Gabriel married in 2005 to Isabel Sarazua and they have two children, Samuel (9) and Asael (4). Five years ago, the Puente family moved to work in Monclova, Coahuila, Mexico, with a small congregation of 14 members. At the end of 2017, Gabriel left that church, to start a new congregation with his family and another sister in the same city.

Bruce Reeves

1. *How and when did you decide to get into preaching full time? What was your motivation or your WHY?*

At a very young age, I had an earnest desire to preach the gospel. I was blessed to grow up in a home with two parents who were extremely faithful and devoted to Christ. I was never pressured to become a preacher, but men who proclaimed the gospel were held in esteem. A number of godly men and women encouraged me to use my talents in teaching the word of God. I did not know of a greater work for the sake of the kingdom of God than sharing the good news of Jesus with the world. I have been blessed to have been encouraged and mentored by dedicated gospel preachers and have always treasured those relationships. My why has always been the joy of glorifying God and helping others grow in their knowledge and fellowship with Christ.

2. *As a preacher, have you always worked in a full-time setting capacity or have you been like Paul building tents from time to time?*

I have always worked in a full-time capacity, but I have always had a great respect for men who worked a secular job and preached the gospel.

3. *What one piece of advice would you give a young man who has begun to preach?*

Study God's Word as a means to spiritual maturity, not simply to preach. Be filled with passion for God's truth and it will naturally flow out of you when you teach.

4. *What wisdom would you give a young man who was thinking about getting into preaching? How can one know when to pull the plug with their decision?*

Receive good counsel from faithful Christians around you about the decision. Commit yourself fully to the work for the Master and never forget whom you are working for in the preaching of Christ, (i.e., the Lord). Love God supremely, but always love the brotherhood. When experienced men of God are concerned that you may not be the most effective in a public capacity, I would re-evaluate my decision.

5. *How do you start your mornings to maximize your day?*

I begin with prayer, personal Bible study, and then I exercise. Then I am ready to pursue my day.

6. *How do you start your week to maximize your time?*

I have sometimes struggled in this area, but I try to use Monday to consider other studies in which I am interested and visit those who may be sick or need encouragement. Then on Tuesday I do my background study for my sermons and Bible studies, and on Thursday I put my work together for Sunday.

7. *What's the biggest challenge you've faced as a preacher? How did you handle it?*

The biggest challenge I have faced is disappointment in brethren in whom I have placed a great deal of confidence. I realize that in those times of difficulty, it is critical to maintain balance in my life as a Christian and balance as a husband and father. I have found absorbing myself in the work of the Lord and in personal devotions in my walk with the Lord orients me in a positive direction.

8. *How does your wife help you in your ministry?*

My wife has been a tremendous blessing to me as a gospel preacher. She encourages me when I may be discouraged, we study and discuss the truth, she offers me an objective perspective about situation, and offers constructive criticism in love. Her example in teaching herself has always been a great exhortation to me personally.

9. *How do you go about writing a sermon? Topic? Length?*

I take several things into consideration. Primarily the needs of the congregation at the time, as well as preceding and subsequent lessons. I also try to balance not only the topics addressed, but also the nature of the lessons. I consult with my shepherds about what they think the needs are for the coming year. I initially do research biblically and take notes, and then I formulate the body of the sermon. Afterward, I arrange a three- to four-page outline. After I have my outline completed, I organize my PowerPoint slides, which helps tighten the lesson.

10. *What book have you gifted the most to people?*

    New Evidence that Demands a Verdict by Josh McDowell.

11. *What are some of your favorite books to read?*

    Inhabiting the Cruciform God by Michael Gorman and *Mere Christianity* by C.S. Lewis.

12. *When do you know when it's time to move to another work?*

    I have found that question challenging. The best advice I have received is that when a significant amount of people who love you are no longer really being changed or influenced by your teaching, it may be time to move. Additionally, it may be that you just realize that you could do more good in the kingdom somewhere else.

13. *What advice would you give to other preachers when it comes to work/family balance?*

    I would encourage you to put a lot of effort into scheduling, organizing, and managing your week. I would also say that you must strive to manage your emotions and mental energy, which is easier to say than to do. It is easy to allow congregational problems to consume you and your family emotionally. I would also say that scheduling time for vacations is critical and planning time with just you and your wife during the week can be very helpful. Additionally, Saturdays may be the day that you need to be able to devote to your wife and children.

14. *Timothy had Paul as a mentor. Who was or is your Paul in the faith? In what ways were they able to help you?*

    I have had several mentors. Elmer Moore, Leon Goff, Lowell Blasingame, Daniel H. King, etc. Really too many to name, but they each have had a different perspective about unique features on the work of preaching the gospel. They have been encouragers and counselors. Most importantly they helped me to form my personal philosophy about preaching the gospel. The most influential lesson from men who have helped me as a gospel preacher is to learn the importance of being true to your convictions and to yourself as you allow the Lord to use you and your personality in His work.

15. *What piece of advice would you give when it comes to evangelism?*

Talk to as many people as you can to diversify potential approaches in sharing the gospel of Christ with the lost. I would take into consideration my culture and environment and the people I am attempting to reach with the truth. Ultimately, allow the example of Christ to guide you in your efforts.

16. *How do you decide how many meetings to hold? When should you decline invitations? How do you go about declining invitations?*

I consult with my shepherds and my wife about how many meetings I should hold. I enjoy being with brethren in various places and have found meetings very helpful to my spiritual growth. When there are concerns that need to be addressed in the local church or it would detrimental to one's family, it would be best to decline an invitation. You can always schedule meetings in the future so that your schedule is manageable. I have had situations in which it just would not be wise to hold a meeting at a particular time. We each must guard our influence wisely. When declining gospel meetings, I think it is important that preachers be specific and honest about the reasoning, balanced with an encouragement for the well-being of the congregation.

Bruce Reeves was born in Blytheville, AR, October 13, 1974, the son of Carl and Carolyn Reeves. He and his wife Rachel have one son, Connor. Bruce received a B.A. degree from Hendrix College and a B. Min degree from Harding University. Bruce has been working with the Highway 65 church of Christ in Conway, AR, for the past 18 years. He has held numerous gospel meetings across the nation. He has written for several religious journals as well. Bruce is active in apologetics in the public forum. Two of the nine formal religious discussions in which he has participated have been published: *The Reeves-Scheel Debate on the Godhead and Baptismal Formula* and the *Reeves-Cook Debate on Baptism*. His books can be found on amazon.com and truthbookstore.com. Bruce loves to read and spend time with his family.

Warren Scholtz

1. *How and when did you decide to get into preaching full time? What was your motivation or your WHY?*

   I was always involved in the church from a child. The congregation where our family worshiped encouraged and trained young men to preach. My father was a preacher in Zimbabwe, and after he was injured in a horse accident, he needed a driver to take him into the villages. I volunteered. I was 30 years old and a qualified cost accountant and also had my own printing business.

   After I had been in the villages, saw the plight of the people, and how evangelist work was needed, that made me sell up everything in the following year and start preaching.

2. *As a preacher, have you always worked in a full-time setting capacity or have you been like Paul building tents from time to time?*

   The first two years of preaching, I supported myself full time, with hunting and farming. I had bought a farm a few years before I started to preach and that helped support me and the family. I still own the farm and still do my tent making and subsidize my support.

3. *What one piece of advice would you give a young man who has begun to preach?*

   Preaching is a hard commitment and you will put yourself and your family in the firing line of many critics. But stay strong, don't be discouraged, and teach the truth without any favor or fear.

4. *What wisdom would you give a young man who was thinking about getting into preaching? How can one know when to pull the plug with their decision?*

   Preach because you love people and serving; don't preach for money or popularity as that wears off very quick. If you cannot handle conflict or sensitive information, or your wife or children do not support your role, STOP.

5. *How do you start your mornings to maximize your day?*

Up at 6 a.m., read the Bible until 6:30, exercise until 7:30, and then breakfast. Read emails and try respond only allowing one hour for this.

6. *How do you start your week to maximize your time?*

Routine is the key to maximize your week. I try to start all my mornings the same except for Sunday or if I am away on a preaching trip. Monday, I like to write a list of all the things that need to be taken care of and block off study times for the week and lesson prep time, so that I have a written plan for the week.

7. *What's the biggest challenge you've faced as a preacher? How did you handle it?*

My biggest challenge continues to be raising support in Africa to preach. It is hard to commit to long-term financial goals as support is never guaranteed. The second is to understand the culture and superstitions in Africa.

8. *How does your wife help you in your ministry?*

My wife is wonderful, always takes care of the children and their needs without me having to worry. My wife also accompanies me to Botswana and is active in teaching the children in the villages.

9. *How do you go about writing a sermon? Topic? Length?*

My sermons are planned on the need or the problems I see in churches. I like to allow brethren to ask questions about anything in the Bible after a study; this way you can tell by questions asked what needs to be taught. A good sermon is no longer than 22–25 min.

10. *What book have you gifted the most to people?*

Corinthians

11. *What are some of your favorite books to read?*

Timothy, James, Acts.

12. *When do you know when it's time to move to another work?*

My work is somehow different than a full-time preacher in the United States. I am constantly moving between congregations and trying to start new works, so I am pretty spread out, which gives me lots of opportunity and challenges to keep me motivated.

13. *What advice would you give to other preachers when it comes to work/family balance?*

Remember that your wife is also a sister in Christ and your children also need time. You as the head need to show them that being a good father and husband is also a requirement of the Bible; they will respect your work more and support you.

14. *Timothy had Paul as a mentor. Who was or is your Paul in the faith? In what ways were they able to help you?*

My mentor and trainer was first my father, and later on it was Clarence Cowart and Max Dawson.

15. *What piece of advice would you give when it comes to evangelism?*

Evangelism is a hard part of preaching. First try to gain people's trust. Don't disregard or discredit their beliefs and faith; try to agree on the Bible as the only source of faith and teach them from the Word gently.

16. *How do you decide how many meetings to hold? When should you decline invitations? How do you go about declining invitations?*

This question is not really applicable in the work I do. We try as the local Mabalabala work to have meetings 2–3 times a year.

Warren Scholtz has been preaching for 18 years in three African countries: South Africa, Zimbabwe, and Botswana. He is married to Ivy Scholtz, and they have 5 children: Anita, Rogan, Damon, Keagan and Josh. His work mainly consists of traveling into remote villages of Africa, converting people, and then establishing churches where there are none. He then continues to train and teach men how to lead in these congregations. He has established 16 new congregations over the last 18 years.

Don Swanson

1. *How and when did you decide to get into preaching full time? What was your motivation or your WHY?*

   I began full-time preaching in 1983 in Port Arthur, TX. I had worked part time in a two-preacher arrangement. The work was so effective I was asked to move to this new location to do full-time work.

2. *As a preacher, have you always worked in a full-time setting capacity or have you been like Paul building tents from time to time?*

   I worked for 21 years for Ford Motor Co. and 15 years of that time I preached as well.

3. *What one piece of advice would you give a young man who has begun to preach?*

   Purchase good reference books. On Monday morning, begin preparing your sermons for the next Sunday. Invite as many people you can find to come hear the sermons you are preparing.

4. *What wisdom would you give a young man who was thinking about getting into preaching? How can one know when to pull the plug with their decision?*

   The advice I was given was, "If you can help it, don't preach."

5. *How do you start your mornings to maximize your day?*

   List the things you need to accomplish for the day. Check them off when accomplished. Begin with the easiest ones first.

6. *How do you start your week to maximize your time?*

   Plan your lessons and the work you wish to accomplish that week on Monday morning.

7. *What's the biggest challenge you've faced as a preacher? How did you handle it?*

Getting the church to understand the importance of the preachers' work. Show them that it can be done.

8. *How does your wife help you in your ministry?*

I do not know how a preacher would do his work effectively without a wife. She serves as his right arm in the work.

9. *How do you go about writing a sermon? Topic? Length?*

I usually have a sermon garden. That is a box filled with ideas I have submitted for future thoughts for sermons. I just let them grow by submitting additional ideas until a three-point sermon develops. Twenty-five minutes is long enough for most preachers.

10. *What book have you gifted the most to people?*

I have written memories entitled *Little Wooden Shoes*. It consists of my preaching for the past 50 years. The price is $15.00. Beginning preachers get it free. If you would like a copy please let me know.

11. *What are some of your favorite books to read?*

I read very little except for information. In my study for sermons and class teaching, I like to see what Homer Hailey has to say.

12. *When do you know when it's time to move to another work?*

More often than not, the brethren tell you. Usually when you have seen personal development on your part and have accomplished the goals set out for the congregation, it is time to move.

13. *What advice would you give to other preachers when it comes to work/family balance?*

A good work ethic is important balanced with a good family life. Both are necessary to your effectiveness.

14. *Timothy had Paul as a mentor. Who was or is your Paul in the faith? In what ways were they able to help you?*

Cecil Belcher showed me by his example that the work of evangelism and can be effective. Johnnie Edwards showed me how to do the work effectively.

15. *What piece of advice would you give when it comes to evangelism?*

Concentrate on one-on-one studies for results. Very few people are converted via the pulpit.

16. *How do you decide how many meetings to hold? When should you decline invitations? How do you go about declining invitations?*

I will hold as many meetings as I consider advantageous to the Lord's work. I only decline if I do not feel I can be of any value to a congregation. I will put a meeting off until a future time. If they continue to call, then I begin to consider going.

Don Swanson was born in McCrory, AR, on September 17, 1941. He graduated from McCrory High School in 1959 and attended Harding University in 1960.

Don began attending services at the McCrory church of Christ with a neighbor lady when he was 12 years old. He soon obeyed the gospel.

In 1961, Don moved to Indiana to find work. He spent 21 years there working for Ford Motor Company. In June 1963, Don married Marsha Dukes. They have two children, Treva Hodge and Trent Swanson.

In 1967, in addition to his full-time job at Ford, he began preaching regularly in Highland, IN. For the next 15 years, he continued to preach in the Northwest Indiana area for congregations in Lowell, Griffith, DeMotte, Gary, and Manteno, IL.

He left his job with Ford in 1983 to move to work with the Stonegate church in Port Arthur, TX. For the next 35 years, he continued to preach for congregations in Silsbee, Liberty, and Mauriceville, TX.

In 2005, Don retired from full-time preaching. Since that time, he has served as a shepherd and evangelist with the Mauriceville Church and also wrote his memoir entitled, *Little Wooden Shoes*.

Ken Weliever

1. *How and when did you decide to get into preaching full time? What was your motivation or your WHY?*

   I was encouraged at a very early age by one of my mentors, Aude McKee. He conducted men's training classes when he was at Plainfield, IN, and encouraged the boys to attend. I began by just saying a memory verse, telling a Bible story, and then a short talk.

   Soon, I was giving invitations on Wednesday night, and by age 16, I was already preaching on an appointment basis for small churches in Central Indiana.

   My parents, Aude, and the church family supplied the motivation to preach through their encouragement and emphasis on the importance of the gospel message and the opportunity and responsibility to use the ability they believed I possessed.

2. *As a preacher, have you always worked in a full-time setting capacity or have you been like Paul building tents from time to time?*

   For most of the past 48 years and I have been fully supported by the local congregations where I preached. There was a period where we supplemented our income through an in-home business.

3. *What one piece of advice would you give a young man who has begun to preach?*

   One piece of advice? That's difficult.

   But maybe this one suggestion will cover a lot of areas. Prepare yourself properly through your own personal growth. The work of the preacher involves so much more than just preaching on Sunday and teaching a class on Wednesday. You must work on your attitude. Grow in leadership. Learn to equip others. And develop relationships. All of that involves preparation and personal, spiritual growth.

4. *What wisdom would you give a young man who was thinking about getting into preaching? How can one know when to pull the plug with their decision?*

Only preach if you can't help it. In other words, don't look at preaching as a career choice of one of many options. You must have the passion and be willing to pay the price because it is calling and a way of life.

5. *How do you start your mornings to maximize your day?*

Coffee. Always coffee. But my activity has changed as I gotten older. For many years, I was not a morning person. But in time, that has changed. Also I've found that it's important to be flexible. For many years, I was pretty strict about working in the church office from 8 or 9 until 4 or 5. As I have gotten older, and with the use of computers that were unavailable when I began, I can do more work at home. But I've found it's best to begin the day with a personal task list of things you need to accomplish. You will get more done that way.

6. *How do you start your week to maximize your time?*

I like to use Monday as a planning day. My wife and I will often go out for breakfast and take our planners to be sure we're on the same page. Speaking of that, I recommend some type of time control devise. I use the system from Franklin-Covey.

7. *What's the biggest challenge you've faced as a preacher? How did you handle it?*

It was being let go from a church that I served for 9 years when it seemed that everything was going fine. The elders didn't present it to me as being fired. They said they just felt it was time for a change. It wasn't anything I had done or not done. That was tough to take. We loved the congregation, the area, the home we lived in, the nature of the work, and the serendipities as a result of the entire situation.

They gave me a 3 1/2 month notice. But it took me almost year to find a place to move. So for 9 months I was unemployed. During my last weeks there, I determined to just preach the Word, continue to minister, refrain from any public or private attacks on the elders, and just let my work speak for itself. People could draw their own conclusions.

To handle something like this, you need to first work hard on your attitude. I had to resist resentment, bitterness, anger, and vindictiveness. Also it easy to feel sorry for yourself. Several close friends helped me through the situation. They helped me network to find another congregation that fit my skill set. They also served as a sympathetic sounding board through the process.

It was during this time, I learned that I wanted to preach whether I was paid or not. This is when I began my blog. It kept me active and gave me an opportunity to engage in a world-wide ministry.

I used the time to refresh, rejuvenate, and revitalize myself. I had a theme song that I listened to several times a day, "Teach Me Lord to Wait."

Also as a piece of advice to young preachers, live on less than you make, so if you're ever in a similar situation, you have savings to fall back on.

8. *How does your wife help you in your ministry?*

My wife, Norma Jean, is the best. She's kind, gracious, tender hearted, and ministry minded. She's always been hospitable and willing to entertain, young and old alike. She's always had a special affinity for the older members and pays extra attention to them. She's great at writing notes, sending out cards for special occasions, and sending thank you notes. She's always been my biggest cheerleader. But she's not afraid to let me know when I messed up, or give me some advice in dealing with some people problem or church issue.

9. *How do you go about writing a sermon? Topic? Length?*

I begin with an idea in mind that I feel has a particular relevance at a given point in time. I consider the needs of the congregation and areas where we need improvement or subjects that are not often covered. I believe, today more than ever, a lot of people are hurting and need encouragement. I try to keep my lessons in the 30-minute range, give or take 5 minutes depending on the topic.

10. *What book have you gifted the most to people?*

Hmm, that's hard to answer. We have given books to young married couples like *His Needs. Her Needs* by Dr. Willard Harley, or other types of marriage books. Usually we try to consider the couple and what might help, so not just one book and it's changed over the years.

I think I could say the same for young people, preachers, elders, and others. I look at their needs and determine what to share. So no one single book stands out.

11. *What are some of your favorite books to read?*

I like to read leadership, church growth, relationship, and personal growth kinds of books. One of my favorite authors is John Maxwell.

12. *When do you know when it's time to move to another work?*

When the church gives you a gift certificate to a moving company for Christmas! Really, that's not something you can quantify by a number of years or some other measurement. It's something you develop a feel for based on many factors.

13. *What advice would you give to other preachers when it comes to work/family balance?*

When I was a young preacher, I saw some older preachers who had worked so hard, held so many meetings, and was gone from home so much that they lost their families. Today divorce is not uncommon even among preachers. I realized that I could not save the world by myself. So I determined to place a high priority on family time. I put in my calendar important events (birthdays, our anniversary, certain holidays) and did not schedule meetings during those times. I didn't schedule Bible studies to conflict with my kids' ball games or recitals. I learned when a person called with something they felt was urgent, that often times it could be scheduled around my family and personal schedule. I've heard preachers brag about not ever taking a vacation. That's not something to brag about. Some of our best family memories revolve around trips we enjoyed together. Also my wife and I have taken time for getaways for just the two of us, and have tried to have a date night once a week. Balance is the key. You do have a family and personal life apart from the work of the church.

14. *Timothy had Paul as a mentor. Who was or is your Paul in the faith? In what ways were they able to help you?*

Growing up, it was Aude McKee. He was one of the best I've ever known with a good combination of pulpit ability, personal evangelism and relationship skills. I learned a lot just by observing him. He was a great encourager to me, even years after I began preaching. Also through the years, I've learned from men like Paul Andrews, Bob Owen, James P. Miller, Robert Jackson, and Dee Bowman. Each possessed a unique skill set in the areas of public speaking, interpersonal relationships, and leadership that has benefitted me greatly.

15. *What piece of advice would you give when it comes to evangelism?*

Be open to opportunities. Some of your best contacts will come through people who visit the services and the friends and relatives of members. I've never had one set of lessons as a one-size-fits-all. Try to meet people where they are and begin with what they know, so you can take them to where they need to be.

16. *How do you decide how many meetings to hold? When should you decline invitations? How do you go about declining invitations?*

In the places where I have preached, the brethren usually restricted my time away to some degree. However, in doing local work plus meeting family responsibilities balanced with personal time away, I've found 8 meetings a year is a pretty reasonable number. I never decline invitations. I will go where ever I am asked. However, I may not be able to come at the time they request, so I will offer an alternative date.

Ken has been preaching the gospel for over 50 years. He began as a high school student preaching on an appointment basis in Central Indiana and continued during his years at Florida College and University of South Florida.

Ken's and his wife, Norma Jean, who will soon be celebrating 50 years of marriage, have lived in seven different states and worked with nine congregations: Park Ave Church, Hillsboro, OH; Kettering Church, Kettering, OH; Palmetto Church, Palmetto, FL; Skyview Church, Pinellas Park, FL; Eastland church, Louisville, KY; Jackson Heights Church, Columbia, TN; North Blvd Church, Tampa, FL; Hickman Mills Church, Kansas City, MO; and West Main Church, Lewisville, TX, where he recently ended full-time work in May 2018. In addition, their travels and ministry have taken them to 49 states, as well as Canada, Mexico, England, Sweden, Denmark, Kazakhstan, and the Virgin Islands.

Currently Ken and Norma Jean are traveling and engaging in national and international ministry as opportunities present themselves in additional to holding gospel meetings.

The Welievers have two grown, married children–Kenny Jr. and Rachél Thompson. They are the proud grandparents of two grandsons and two granddaughters.

Ken publishes a daily devotional blog, www.ThePreachersWord.com.

The Message These Men Preach

I've been privileged to personally know the men who have helped contribute to this book. I have had the opportunity to spend time with them, to study with them, to hear them teach and preach. I'm truly thankful to know them. But it could be the case that you may not know these men. It could also be the case you don't know the message these men preach. I would like to share that message with you.

All of these men preach the same message. They preach the same message because there's only one faith. The apostle Paul said in Ephesians 4:4–6, "There is one body and one Spirit just as you were called to the one hope that belongs to your call, one Lord, one faith, one baptism, one God and Father of all, who is over all and through all and in all." They preach that there is one God and Father of all. They preach and encourage men and women to believe in the God of Abraham, Isaac, and Jacob. They preach what the Hebrew writer says in Hebrews 11:6, "And without faith it is impossible to please him, for whoever draws near to God must believe that He exists and that He rewards those who seek Him."

These men preach about the love, mercy, grace, holiness, and justice of God. They proclaim that God sent His Son Jesus to the world to save man from our sins, John 3:16. They proclaim that Jesus is both Lord and Christ, Acts 2:36. These gospel preachers teach and preach the good news of Jesus. Because Jesus lived a sinless life, because He died on the cross, and rose from the grave on the first day of the week, we can have hope! We can have hope of eternal life. We can have hope of being delivered from our sins. We can have hope of having peace with the God of peace through the Prince of peace. That's good news. True hope is only found in Jesus. That's what these men believe and proclaim. They preach that by grace we are saved from our sins, Ephesians 2:8-9. As gospel preachers, they proclaim that God's grace is available to all who will obey the Father. The apostle Paul reminded the disciples in Romans 6:17-18, "But thanks be to God, that you who were once slaves of sin have become obedient from the heart to the standard of teaching to which you were committed, and having been set free sin, have become slaves of righteousness." The saints in Rome believed in the resurrection of Jesus from the grave, Romans 1:4. They believed He is the Son of God. They obeyed from the heart the standard of teaching delivered to them and were baptized, <u>Romans 6:4-7.</u> They obeyed the words of Jesus and were baptized for the forgiveness of sins, <u>Mark 16:16</u>. All men can be saved by God's amazing grace. No one deserves His grace. Paul would say in <u>Romans 6:23</u>, "For the wages of sin is death, but the free gift of God is eternal life in Christ Jesus our Lord." This is what these men preach. This is what they believe. They believe Christians should continue to grow in the grace and knowledge of our Lord and Savior and continue steadfastly in the apostles' doctrine, the breaking of bread, fellowship, and prayer as we await the second coming of our Lord and Savior.

Made in the USA
San Bernardino, CA
26 August 2018